Keep 2/09

W9-BRK-368

ALSO BY NAT HENTOFF

Peace Agitator: The Story of A. J. Muste

The New Equality

Call the Keeper

Our Children Are Dying

Onwards

A Doctor Among the Addicts

Hear Me Talkin' to Ya (with Nat Shapiro)

Journey Into Jazz

A Political Life: The Education of John V. Lindsay

In the Country of Ourselves

State Secrets: Police Surveillance in America

The Jazz Life (with Paul Cowan and Nick Egleson)

Jazz Is

Does Anybody Give a Damn?
Nat Hentoff on Education

The First Freedom: The Tumultuous History of
Free Speech in America

The Day They Came to Arrest the Book

Boston Boy: A Memoir

John Cardinal O'Connor: At the Storm Center of a
Changing American Catholic Church

Blues for Charlie Darwin

The Man from Internal Affairs

Free Speech for Me—But Not for Thee:
How the American Left & Right Relentlessly
Censor Each Other

listen TO THE stories

NAT HENTOFF ON JAZZ AND COUNTRY MUSIC

NAT HENTOFF

HarperCollins*Publishers*

HarperCollins books may be purchased for educational, business, or sales promotional use. For information please write: Special Markets Department, HarperCollins Publishers, Inc., 10 East 53rd Street, New York, NY 10022.

FIRST EDITION

Designed by Nancy Singer

Library of Congress Cataloging-in-Publication Data

Hentoff, Nat.
   Listen to the stories : Nat Hentoff on jazz and country music / Nat Hentoff.
     p. cm.
   In part rev. versions of articles previously published in the Wall Street
Journal's "Leisure & Arts" section.
   Includes bibliographical references and index.
   ISBN 0-06-019047-7
   1. Jazz—History and criticism. 2. Country music—History and criticism. I. Title
ML3507.H46 1995
781.65'09—dc20   95-1395

95 96 97 98 99 ❖/RRD 10 9 8 7 6 5 4 3 2 1

For my son Tom, who imagined this book. And for
Ray Sokolov, editor of the *Wall Street Journal's*
"Leisure & Arts" page—but for whom this book would
not exist because earlier versions of some of these
choruses first appeared on his page.
Also, this book is in gratitude to Charles Mingus, who
taught me about much more than music.

You could walk down the street, open a door for two seconds, and say, "Oh yeah, that's Lockjaw." Or you walk down to the next club and say, "Oh yeah, that's Sonny Rollins." You know who's playing. But to me, right now, during this time, a lot of people have lost that idea of having a signature sound. Still, when you get to be about thirty or thirty-five years old, you should be developing into your own sound, but now they've gone for excessive notes. If you're not at the point of developing into your own sound, there's something wrong, and you have chosen a path that is not an individual one.

—David Murray

Don't play what's there, play what's not there.

—Miles Davis

If the rhythm section ain't making it, go for yourself.

—Ben Webster

Just make it, baby, make it very soft and low
If you will make it, baby, make it very soft and low
If you feel like lying down
With me on the pallet on the floor
When your main girl come
I swear, she will never know

—Mama and Jimmy Yancey

contents

INTRODUCTION

It was a little before ten in the morning on a dark Saturday. The rain had been coming down so hard so long that subways and streets were flooded. On the West Side of Manhattan a number of black men, carrying instrument cases and grumbling at both the rain and the eerie time of day, began gathering in a rehearsal studio. In the evening they were to be part of a tribute to Count Basie at Carnegie Hall.

Most of the musicians were in their sixties and seventies. Contrary to the myth nurtured for a time by white novelists, jazz is by no means exclusively a young man's game. On hand that morning, for instance, was the most deeply, resiliently swinging drummer in all of jazz, Gus Johnson, now in his seventies. His lithe and crisp appearance led an onlooker—my daughter—to say, "Jazz sure keeps you young."

As with most of the other players that day, Gus Johnson's name is known only to other musicians and to the true aficionados around the world. He and everyone else in the studio had played with Count Basie at one time or another.

They started to run down some arrangements scored for that night, but trumpeter Harry "Sweets" Edison stopped the music. Too many notes. There had to be more space. Sweets devoutly believes, as did Basie, that less is more. The fewer notes you play—provided you know why each one is there—the more you'll swing and the clearer story you'll tell. So Sweets told the arranger, standing there, that he was going to take a bunch of notes out of his part and he was also going to slow down the tempo. There was no point arguing with Sweets. He'd spent all those nights with Basie. The arranger hadn't been on even one road trip.

The power of space was not only Basie's credo. Dizzy Gillespie used to say, "It's taken me all my life to know what not to play."

Around noon another group of Basie alumni arrived to rehearse what everybody was calling the Reno Club set. As with the previous band, they greeted one another with the kind of warmth that comes from making serious joyful music together over a long time, no matter how many years ago. It's stronger than many family ties.

The Reno Club had been a place in Kansas City where Basie, way back, had led a nine-piece band that by all accounts swung more exuberantly and surely than any in jazz history. Those were the years when the sounds of jazz never stopped in Kansas City. You could hear the brass shout any time, day or night.

And the brass were shouting again that gray morning. I had brought my daughter—a pianist, singer, and composer—to the rehearsal because, though she had worked with many of the young jazz players in town, she had never been in the presence of jazz elders. After a couple of hours, she said, "I've never seen such *love* among musicians before."

One late winter afternoon when I was sixteen, I was on my way to a jazz record store when I walked past the Savoy Café, in a black neighborhood of Boston. The club was closed, but the blues coming from inside stopped me. I looked through the glass high up in the door and saw a tenor saxophonist with a huge swaggering sound, sitting on a chair that was leaning back against a table. I looked again. It *was* Coleman Hawkins.

The pianist's every note was placed to give the big tenor a further lift. And every one of those notes from Count Basie's piano seemed to make the room move. There was a drummer, uncommonly subtle, whose eyes darted from player to player. His brushes were dancing on the drumhead, punctuated by an occasional deep sigh from a cymbal. That, I knew, had to be Basie's drummer, Jo Jones, whom musicians described as "the man who plays like the wind."

There was no one else there. The musicians wore their hats, as many of them did in those days during rehearsals and jam sessions. I stayed for a long time looking through the glass in the door listening to them talk to one another in the blues.

It grew dark, the lights went on, and the music stopped, but not for me.

Once in a while I'm asked by a student at a high school or college what I consider my most lasting achievement. A television program, I tell them, "The Sound of Jazz" on CBS-TV one Sunday afternoon in 1957.

The producer, Robert Herridge, was the most original and stubborn force in television history. I was first aware of how much he could do with sheer obsessive integrity when I saw, years before, WCBS-TV's "Camera Three," a three-part adaptation of *Notes from Underground*. There was no set. Just an actor and a chair. This was full-strength Dostoyevsky, as penetrating as a Roy Eldridge solo.

Herridge insisted on keeping whatever he did—from an hour with the Philadelphia Orchestra to *All the King's Men* to "The Sound of Miles Davis"—pure. "*Partisan Review* pure" is how he put it.

He'd always wanted to create a pure jazz program, and he asked Whitney Balliett of *The New Yorker* and me to select the musicians and work with them on the numbers to be played. There were to be no sets. The bare studio and the cameras would be the only backdrops for the musicians. On the basis of his experience with cameramen on previous shows, Herridge picked those who could improvise. He told them to not worry about being caught in someone else's shot. The audience would know they were there anyway. And whenever they saw a particularly arresting shot, they were to take it—not wait for the control room.

The musicians were told to dress as they would for a rehearsal, even at the ultimate performance, which—as was the case in those days—would be filmed live. That meant most of the musicians wore their hats. Later, this was to bring a very dignified and singular jazz musician, Benny Carter, to excoriate me for letting those jazzmen into living rooms all over America with their hats on. I thought the hats were quite distinctive.

Billie Holiday had not remembered my telling her that the show had no sets and that she was to dress in whatever was most comfortable for her. She was furious at me, and at a sound check she snapped, "I bought a goddamn five-hundred-dollar dress for this show!"

Among the musicians, along with Billie, were Coleman Hawkins, Lester Young, Ben Webster, Jo Jones, Count Basie, Thelonious Monk, Jimmy Rushing, Henry "Red" Allen, Roy Eldridge, Rex Stewart, Doc Cheatham, Dicky Wells, Pee Wee Russell, Gerry Mulligan, and Jimmy Giuffre.

They played with extraordinary passion and swing—in part because they were on live national television but mainly because they were unmistakably in the company of their peers and very much wanted to impress them.

Throughout the hours of getting the lighting and sound right, Herridge never suggested that we replace any of the lesser-known musicians—many of whom had never before been on national television—with more "box office" names.

The program, part of a "Seven Lively Arts" series, was commercially sponsored. At one point, a representative of the sponsor told Herridge it would not be seemly to have a woman who had been busted on drug charges entering America's homes, especially on a Sunday afternoon. Herridge said the problem could be resolved very quickly. If the sponsor did not back down, Herridge, Hentoff, and Balliett would leave the program. He spoke the truth. Billie Holiday stayed.

When "The Sound of Jazz" was on the air, we in the control room were moving in time to the music until something happened that nobody had anticipated. It was an epiphany, a wordless remembrance of things past between Lester Young ("Prez" she had nicknamed him long ago) and Billie Holiday ("Lady Day" had been his name for her).

They had once been very close, but for reasons unknown they had grown far apart. During the week before airtime they had avoided each other. And Lester Young, sick and weak, had to be replaced on the big-band numbers. All he had left was Billie's number. I told him before the show started that he didn't have to stand up for his solo; he could stay seated.

Billie was seated on a stool, and in a semicircle around her were the musicians. She began to sing. In the control room we leaned forward. The song, "Fine and Mellow," was one of the few blues in her repertory. She sang about trouble long in mind, with some kicks along the way. Her sound was tart, tender, knowing. And she was sinuously swinging.

It was time for Prez. He stood up and played the sparest, purest blues chorus I have ever heard. Nodding, smiling, Billie was inside the music. Her eyes met his. It was as if they were in another, familiar place, a very private place. I felt tears, and so did Herridge.

When the program was over and I was standing in the wings, I saw Billie coming toward me. She said nothing about the five-hundred-dollar dress. She just kissed me. It was the best award I've ever gotten.

Many letters came in from around the country about that program, and Herridge read them with great pleasure. They confirmed his conviction that there were a lot of people out there who could take art straight. And pure. A woman from White Plains, New York, wrote as soon as "The Sound of Jazz" was over to say that "one so seldom has the chance to see real people doing something that really matters to them."

Years later, the Museum of Broadcasting in New York had a showing of "The Sound of Jazz," followed by a discussion involving some of us who had been involved in the program.

A young man asked me: "How were you able to get so many great players in one place at the same time?"

"They could all use the gig," I said.

PART I
diminuendo and
crescendo in blue

DUKE ELLINGTON,
1899–1974

During more than thirty years of knowing Duke, I hardly ever saw anger in him. That is, overt, visible anger. It did come through once when we were talking about putting labels on music.

"Riding in the car with Harry Carney the other night," Duke said, "I heard a cat on the radio talking about what he called 'modern jazz.' So he played a record to illustrate his point. And you know, there were devices in that music I heard cats using in the nineteen twenties.

"Those large words like *modern* don't *mean* anything," Ellington said sharply. "Anybody who has had anything to say in this music—all the way back—has been an individualist. I mean musicians like Sidney Bechet, Louis Armstrong, Coleman Hawkins. Then what happens is that hundreds of other musicians begin to be shaped by that one man. They fall in behind him, and you've got what people call a category. But I don't listen in terms like 'modern' jazz. I listen for those individualists. Like Charlie Parker was."

When Duke wanted to praise someone—which he did, I thought, nondiscriminately out of chronic kindness—he would often say that the musician or singer being talked about was "beyond category." In all of American music, there has been no one but Duke to whom that term, "beyond category," can be applied with total accuracy. Of course, he had roots, but what he created over half a century was a microcosm, a musical universe all his own. His own and that of his musicians. No other band could play Duke's charts and sound at all like his orchestra did. Not even that of Charlie Barnet, who idolized him so.

One reason for the utter singularity of that universe was, of course, that Duke wrote for specific musicians. "I know," he once told me, "what each man does best, what his strengths are, what his capacities are, and I write to that." That's why when someone who had been with Duke for a long time left to go out on his own, he always sounded somehow incomplete in the outer world. Some recognized that and came back, having learned that Duke could find qualities in a musician he didn't know he had.

The microcosm could not be copied for another reason. It was part of an extraordinarily cohesive continuum. Like Bach, Duke worked in a multitude of forms, transmuting them, interrelating them all to a huge body of work with its own logic of evolution, expansion, and continual regeneration. No piece by Duke was ever finished. When I was a kid, going to hear him night after night at dances in Boston, then later being allowed by him to come to rehearsals, I kept hearing songs going through all sorts of changes. Sidemen would make suggestions, some of which Duke would accept. And he would have a new idea and put it in.

Years might go by before the piece was played, and suddenly—if Tom Whaley, the librarian of Ellingtonia, could find it—it would reappear, to be changed yet again.

By then there were new players in the band who in turn would generate new ideas in Duke. And yet the new and the old were part of that wholly distinctive continuum, that microcosm that this one man, and only he, controlled.

No wonder Duke would get exasperated by people trying to put labels on music, especially his music. There was the music of Ellington, and there was other music. And because his musicians were so integral a part of how he wanted to express himself, Duke was intensely loyal to them. A good many years ago, he roared—an extreme rarity—at a young man who was then head of *Down Beat*'s Chicago office. In Duke's band at the time was a heroin addict, and that night he had nodded off during the whole first set.

"It looks awful, Duke," the young critic said, "that guy zonked out in public. Why don't you get rid of him?"

"Do you realize," Duke said furiously, "that that man fought for you in the South Pacific where he contracted a rare form of malaria which puts him in this condition from time to time?"

The blood of the musician in question would have instantly stunned any mosquito to death, but Duke was not about to have a citizen of his own principality criticized by an outsider.

Duke could not fire a man. "What he does," Billy Strayhorn once told me, "is wait until it becomes obvious to the man himself that he'd be happier somewhere else. And sooner or later, the man leaves." Duke did fire one man though—Charles Mingus. He had just joined the orchestra, which was playing at the Apollo Theater in Harlem. Backstage, trombonist Juan Tizol was criticizing the bassist for having misplayed a piece that Tizol had written. Mingus, whose temper was just as quick, chased Tizol away. But as the curtain rose with the band playing its buoyant theme, "Take the A Train," Tizol, wielding a bolo knife, could be seen at the back of the stage lunging at Mingus.

What happened next was described by Mingus to me, and later by him in print. In capturing not only the elaborately euphemistic language of Ellington, Mingus also caught the very cadences of his speech when, unable to avoid unpleasantness, Ellington tried to make the distracting dissonance gently disappear.

"'Now, Charles,' Ellington said to Mingus, looking amused, putting Cartier links into the cuffs of his beautiful hand-made shirt, 'you could have forewarned me—you left me out of the act entirely! At least you could have let me cue in a few chords as you ran through that Nijinsky routine.

"'I congratulate you on your performance, but why didn't you and Juan inform me about the adagio you planned, so that we could score it? I must say I never saw a large man so agile—I never saw *anybody* make such tremendous leaps! The gambado over the piano carrying your bass was colossal.

"'When you exited after that, I thought, "That man's really afraid of Juan's knife, and at the speed he's going he's probably home in bed by now." But no, back you came through the same door with your bass still intact. For a moment I was hopeful you'd decided to sit down and play, but instead you slashed Juan's chair in two with a fire axe!

"'Really, Charles, that's destructive. Everybody knows Juan has a knife, but nobody ever took it seriously—he likes to pull it out and show it to people, you understand. So I'm afraid, Charles—I've never fired anybody—you'll have to quit my band. I don't need any new problems. Juan's an old problem. I can cope with that, but you seem to have a whole bag of new tricks. I must ask you to be kind enough to give me your notice, Mingus.'"

A musician who was in the band at the time told me, "I was amazed that Duke actually did fire Mingus. I thought he'd wait at least until Mingus had split Juan Tizol's head open."

Musicians outside the band were never criticized by Duke. "I'm not good at appraisals," he would say. But if he liked someone, he would try to help in his oblique, courtly way. English pianist Marian McPartland, new in America, was playing at the Hickory House in New York, where Ellington often dined when he was in the city. Marian came down after a set, and Duke said, with a large smile, "You play so many notes." It took several months for that to sink in. "I was green as grass," Marian remembers. "Then I realized he was telling me to edit myself and play music rather than notes."

There was that Duke, and there was always the man who was highly aware and proud of his blackness. He wrote "Black Beauty" in 1928, in tribute to Florence Mills. And through the years, there were the show *Jump for Joy*, the long works ("Black, Brown and Beige," "Deep South Suite," "My People"), and many more explorations and celebrations of the black heritage.

We were talking once about black consciousness, and Duke mentioned that in the 1920s, when Paul Whiteman was allegedly bringing "dignity" to jazz, Duke went to Fletcher Henderson and said, "Why don't we drop the word *jazz*? We ought to call what we're doing 'Negro music.' Then there won't be any confusion." Henderson preferred not to.

Duke also pointed out how, long before the civil rights movement, he never allowed himself or his men to be treated with disrespect. Take for example their 1934–36 tour of the Deep South. "We did it," said Duke, "without the benefit of federal judges, and we commanded respect. We didn't travel by bus. Instead we had two Pullman cars and a seventy-foot baggage car. We parked them in each station and lived in them. We had our own water, food, electricity, and sanitary facilities. The natives would come by and say, 'What's that?' 'Well,' we'd say, 'that's the way the President travels.'"

When he was with other presidents, Duke was never awed, being of higher rank. Toward the end of Lyndon Johnson's presidency he was part of the group on a cross-country plane ride so that Lady Bird could say good-bye to America. The plane was full of security personnel, and Duke, at one point, leaned over to a political figure he knew and whispered, "Would you like some grass?"

Ellington always had great presence, off as well as on the stand, and he delighted in saying, straight-faced, things that would softly throw his listeners off stride. He took pleasure in occasionally making it difficult for those he met to know whether and when to take him seriously.

I found out, for instance, that the best way to interview Ellington was on the phone. We'd had an appointment to meet one day, but I was sick and called him instead. The interview lasted more than an hour, and it was the most illuminating—about how he worked as a leader and composer—that I'd ever had with him. Alone, he wasn't "on," he wasn't performing. He was serious.

Oddly, although he was held in worldwide respect as an orchestra leader and composer, Ellington was largely underestimated as a pianist by his public here and abroad—not only as a soloist but as an accompanist for the band as a whole as well as for soloists.

Yet, as a soloist in the celebratory Harlem stride piano tradition—with bold harmonies, silvery melodies, and unexpected rhythms, all of which presaged Thelonious Monk—Ellington could have held recitals all by himself. Furthermore, as Dizzy Gillespie once said, "there's never been a comper [accompanist] as good as Duke."

He was also a master of the put-on. Toward the end of his time, I was standing at the back of a New York club, listening to the band. For some reason, Duke was not on the stand. I felt a hand on my shoulder, and then I heard the voice.

"You don't know who I am," Edward Kennedy Ellington said, "but *I* know who *you* are."

Just about everybody knew who Duke was. He touched many lives in ways that he could never have known about. On the street outside his funeral at the august Cathedral of Saint John the Divine in New York, a black man, a resident of Harlem, said, "I'm just here to bear witness. A man passed through, and he was a giant."

"I think," Miles Davis said, "all the musicians in jazz should get together on a certain day and get down on their knees to thank Duke."

THE DUKE, IN PRIVATE

In their range of emotions, forms, and probes into the experiences of black Americans, Duke Ellington's works are as serious as American music has ever been.

Yet it was hard to relate the public Ellington—ever smiling, never showing the merest twinge of anger, repeating "I love you madly" like a silly mantra—to the depth and complexity of the music.

One of the few times I saw Ellington without his impenetrable public mask was when he lost what turned out to be his last chance for a Pulitzer Prize—a token special award for his "total production." But the overall Pulitzer board didn't think he was worth even that handout and reversed the music jury.

In public, smiling broadly, the sixty-six-year-old Ellington dismissed the humiliation as if it could never have possibly happened: "Fate doesn't want me to be too famous too young."

A couple of nights later, Ellington, coldly angry, told me, "Well, you see, most Americans still take it for granted that European-based music—classical music, if you will—is the only really respectable kind. What we do, what other black musicians do, has always been like the kind of man you wouldn't want your daughter to associate with."

Until now, the few television documentaries on Ellington have largely focused on performances of the public man and his music. None has been able to reveal much about the private Ellington, the Ellington who could be angry. But *Reminiscing in Tempo* (part of PBS's "American Experience" series) does finally illuminate more of Ellington offstage than has been caught on film before.

The sixty-minute expedition moves past the lore and into the obsessive priorities of the man behind the legend. (A companion CD is available on Columbia/Legacy.) It is a kaleidoscope of the orchestra in performance, Ellington rehearsing, Ellington being interviewed—and unusually candid comments by friends, colleagues, and members of the family.

The worldly Marian Logan, widow of Dr. Arthur Logan, Ellington's longtime physician and closest friend, said, "Duke was the most completely selfish person I've ever known. Also the most generous."

Ellington greatly enjoyed women, and they enjoyed him, but as Marian Logan noted, they all "made the one fatal mistake of believing that they were the one. And there was no such animal. The one with Edward was his music."

Even in the leanest times, he had to have his orchestra so he could hear what he wrote as soon as it was on paper. To keep that costly necessity intact required a lot of charm and manipulation. For a long time Irving Mills, an aggressive music publisher, booked the band, orchestrated its publicity, and "cowrote" many Ellington originals, including "Mood Indigo." Accordingly, as Mercer Ellington, Duke's son, says on the program, "Mills got half the composer's end and was also the publisher, and therefore he got all the publisher's end. So Ellington got fifteen percent of the tune while Irving got seventy-five."

As a youngster, I used to wonder why Ellington needed help from this otherwise unknown songwriter, and when members of the band finally told me the story, I wondered even more that Ellington, so proud and independent, allowed himself to be exploited. But Mills's business acumen gave the band some financial stability, and Ellington was willing to sacrifice even his pride for that.

He finally dissolved the partnership with Mills when he

found out that although he had told Mills to buy a five-thousand-dollar casket when Ellington's mother died, Mills had bought a cheaper model. There was no one in his life whom Ellington loved more than his mother. He used to say she wouldn't let his feet touch the ground until he was seven.

The assertion is made by friends on the program that Ellington, so absorbed in his music, never thought about civil rights. Yet during the 1960s, when he was criticized by some young black activists for not joining in the struggle, he was very hurt—privately. "They've not been listening to our music," he told me. "For a long time, social protest and pride in black culture and history have been the most significant themes in what we've done. In that music we have been talking for a long time about what it is to be black in this country." ("Duke was a historian," Dizzy Gillespie told me years later.)

And on *Reminiscing in Tempo* itself there is a newspaper head-line about Ellington, having been refused service in a Baltimore restaurant, joining with students in protest and saying, "Well, it all boils down to the skin disease, more or less."

Ellington was a major hypochondriac, with a huge collection of symptoms. In his last years, he devoted much of his time to cre-ating sacred music. Though urgent, the compositions seemed thin to me, and I thought he was building credits up there in case any-thing happened to him down here. But it was this life to which he remained fiercely attached; and even when Dr. Logan found he had incurable cancer, Ellington figured that Logan would some-how find a way to keep him on the road. But then Logan died suddenly, and despite all that religious music he had written, Ellington was in despair, telling Marian Logan, "I won't last six months."

Five months later, he died. He had stayed on the road with the band until he was hospitalized. He had to hear the music. And he had to hear and feel the listeners.

The public "I love you madly" Ellington kept charming the audiences because he felt that was one way to show his gratitude that they were there. As *Reminiscing in Tempo* shows by intercut-ting between what Ellington lived for and how he kept it going, he also believed that private feelings were just that.

His Boswell, Stanley Dance, tells of the Ellington band's first trip to Argentina: "He had played his final concert and sat in the car outside the theater before going to the airport. People clutched at him through the open windows, people who were crying, who thrust gifts on him, gifts on which they hadn't even written their names. It was one of the few times I saw him moved to tears."

DANCING WITH THE DUKE, I

From the time I was twelve, my greatest pleasures in Boston were watching Ted Williams effortlessly hit baseballs enormous distances and hearing Duke Ellington play at dances. Both men had great presence, but Williams was a loner while Ellington thrived in the company of dancing strangers. "If I hear a sigh of pleasure from the dance floor," he once told me, "it becomes part of our music."

In concert halls and nightclubs Ellington was always intriguing, sometimes mysteriously so. But the orchestra was—and had—the most fun at dances. The players got an immediate and continual physical response from the dancers, and that gave them more energy, more enjoyment in giving palpable pleasure. I used to stay all night, my chin on the bandstand as close as I could get; and when an unfamiliar number was played, I'd ask Harry Carney, the burly and kindly baritone saxophone player, what the piece was called. Usually he'd shake his head; the song was so new, all it had was a number.

There have been a number of recordings of Ellington dance dates, but for years the most prized of all had been made in Fargo, North Dakota, in 1940. The first version, *Duke Ellington in Fargo, North Dakota*, was uneven in sound quality, but the band was so buoyant, so loose without ever losing their way, that it was as if everybody were partying. The recording went out of print for some years, becoming available again from time to time on different labels.

The original recording was made by Dick Burris and Jack Towers. Based at different colleges in North Dakota, each had recording experience with Farm Radio. They came to the dance to get the band on acetate for their own pleasure. "I certainly never thought," Jack Towers told me years later, "that people would be listening to this fifty years in the future."

The acetates were played about six hundred to seven hundred times in the following years, and the heavy pickups and steel needles of the time plowed out much of the soft grooves. But the set has recently been restored by Mr. Towers, who is now renowned throughout the world for his skill—by using various-sized styli and other restorative equipment—in bringing seemingly dead grooves back to life. Each project takes an extraordinary amount of time, and Mr. Towers keeps resolving to cut down on his assignments. But it's hard, since he delights in the challenge and, of course, the music.

The still-vivid Fargo night, half a century ago, took place at the Crystal Ballroom, a large hall with very good acoustics. The band had come in by train that afternoon. The musicians were on a characteristically grueling series of Ellington one-nighters. The November 7 Fargo date had been preceded that month by engagements in Muncie, Illinois; East Grand Forks, Michigan; and Winnipeg, Manitoba; as well as by recording sessions in Chicago. The trip from Winnipeg to Fargo had taken about eight hours, and the players looked tired as they drifted into the Crystal Ballroom.

"But you can't tell what's going to happen on any given night on the road," one of Ellington's musicians once told me. "You can come into some place, you don't even remember the name, beat to the socks. But then, on the stand, something happens and you're wide awake and ready to go. Other times, nothing happens, and you just play the notes."

Something happened that night in Fargo, and fortunately— with the Farm Radio engineers there—it happened to the most accomplished assembly of original soloists Ellington ever headed: alto saxophonist Johnny Hodges; tenor saxophonist Ben Webster (in one of his most majestic evenings); the pungent, epigrammatic Tricky Sam Nanton on trombone; Lawrence Brown, the most lyrically intimate of trombonists when he was not strutting gloriously through the brass; and trumpeter Ray Nance, who had just joined the band and hardly knew the book but you couldn't tell.

Another singular improviser was cornetist Rex Stewart, a musician of exceptional energy, mocking wit, bristling intelligence, and a passion for taking risks. I heard him often during those years, but on this night he may well have even surprised himself. Also present was Jimmy Blanton, with whom modern bass playing began; clarinetist Barney Bigard, who played as if he were calling to his beloved on some far shore; the robustly dependable Carney on baritone saxophone; and Sonny Greer, who approached the drums as if he were doing a magic act.

The repertory includes such standards of the band (never played quite the same way twice) as "Ko-Ko," "Harlem Airshaft," "Warm Valley," "Rumpus in Richmond," and "Rose of the Rio Grande."

Singing from time to time were Herb Jeffries (with an erotically large and gentle sound) and Ivie Anderson. Of all Ellington's vocalists, she was the most impudently independent and original.

There are valuable notes by Andrew Homzy, and in them he tells of recording engineers Jack Towers and Dick Burris, an hour after the music ended, listening to some of the acetates. Mr. Burris looked at Mr. Towers and said, "We don't realize what we have here." They were beginning to.

The day before, during a newspaper interview in Winnipeg, Duke Ellington spoke of his desire to establish "an unadulterated American Negro music." He sure did.

DANCING WITH THE DUKE, II

Ellington was delighted, he once told me, to always have musicians on hand so that he could hear almost immediately what he had composed and then be able to keep recomposing it. And he was sorry for those classical composers who "hear a premiere and then have to put the score in the drawer."

Often, however, the Ellington dances would begin with just a pianist. The sidemen were habitual latecomers, and the stars of the band vied with one another as to who would be the latest, and therefore the most independent, of all. So while waiting, Duke, who seldom played extended solos with the band, would return to the high-spirited two-handed stride piano of his youth or gently pursue a fragile intimation of a tune that might, hundreds of miles and many nights later, emerge as an Ellington standard.

Once the band was in place, it was sometimes exhilaratingly clear how the musicians coming off the bus, sleepy and cranky with yet another trip through the dawn after a gig, could be regenerated by the dancers.

"You're giving them something to move by," an Ellington sideman once explained to me, "but they're giving you something back. You can tell whether you're really cooking by how they move on the floor, and when they groove, they make you groove more."

For a cracklingly immediate sense of what it was like to be at an Ellington dance, there are two volumes of *Duke Ellington/All Star Road Band* (Doctor Jazz Records). The first was recorded in Carrolltown, Pennsylvania, a small agricultural town in the Alleghenies, in June 1957. The second makes permanent a one-nighter at the Holiday Ballroom in Chicago, a high-ceilinged former theater, in May 1964.

On both sets the Ellington presence is compelling. On piano he was a masterful accompanist, lighting the way for soloists and joyously driving the band to keep discovering more of what was in his scores. A corollary dimension of the Ellington presence was his verbal accompaniment of the players. It was considerably less restrained at dances than at concerts, and it usually came at those incandescent moments when a soloist or the full orchestra was just about to levitate musically.

At the Carrolltown dance, the numbers range from "Take the A Train" and "Sophisticated Lady" to "Such Sweet Thunder" from Ellington's Shakespeare suite. Among the soloists is Johnny Hodges, the most sensuous alto saxophonist in the history of the music so far. There was never a hint of effort in his soaring playing. Indeed, it looked as if the instrument played itself. And at this dance, there is a "Jeep's Blues" by Hodges that is a classic illustration, as Stanley Dance says in the notes, of what jazz musicians mean by "telling a story."

Toward the end of the Carrolltown dance, Duke reminds the patrons that "the bar will close at one o'clock tonight. We regret to tell you that we will be here a half hour later though. So if you're going to be with us, let's be fortified."

Is this what a distinguished composer, one of America's most original, should be doing? Ellington didn't mind. It was part of the business, the business that allowed him to be on the road enough nights to pay what he called "these expensive gentlemen" who traveled with him. What was making a bar call compared with the luxury of having those musicians very much in mind when by himself he sketched out a new piece much later that night?

Volume II of the *Road Band* sets, the Chicago date, reveals Ellington the disciplinarian. Actually, as noted, he had an enormous distaste for unpleasantness and hardly ever fired anybody. But if he saw a musician return from a rather too enthusiastic trip to the bar during intermission, Ellington would often immediately call a number featuring that musician. And then yet another solo showcase for the not-too-steady soul. And sometimes a third solo in a row. Usually, the player would bump into some notes, to his discomfiture and to the grins of his colleagues.

This form of punishment happens to Johnny Hodges at the Chicago dance. It was impossible for Hodges to play a poor solo, but it is intriguing to hear the mildly inebriated saxophonist doing just a little slipping and sliding, although he always recovers.

Among the many pleasures of the date is trombonist Lawrence Brown's stretching out. At concerts Brown looked and spoke like the headmaster of an exclusive preparatory school and was very self-disciplined. But at a dance he could play a roaringly unbuttoned, lusty gutbucket horn (as on "Do Nothin' Till You Hear from Me" here).

When he was in his sixties, I once asked Duke, who had just returned from a long, grueling tour, why, since his ASCAP royalties were considerable, he didn't retire from the ardors of the road.

He looked at me in annoyed astonishment. "Retire to what?"

THE SENSUALIST

When alto saxophonist Charlie Parker overturned the jazz scene in the 1940s, a young associate of his said triumphantly that Bird had made all the swing-era players immediately outdated. Although this was predictable revolutionary hyperbole, it is true that some swing-era musicians—on all instruments—were confused and bitter as modern jazz (or bop) received more and more attention. There were sad and angry older musicians who thought they actually had been passed by.

An imperturbable exception was Johnny Hodges, Duke Ellington's magisterial alto saxophonist since 1928. He was, as Ellington said, beyond category. Hodges played as if he were singing; his effortless, soaring sound was both powerful and intimate; and swinging was as natural to him as speaking—probably more so, since Hodges was notably laconic, as cautious with words as Count Basie, who was also a master of time.

Hodges and Charlie Parker were deeply alike in one respect. Throughout their careers, both were constantly nurtured by the blues. As Dizzy Gillespie has said, "Johnny Hodges is a blues player, quiet as it's kept. He could moan a while." But Hodges's blues—and there were blues textures and inflections in just about everything he played—were not the shouting kind. And they were not despairing blues. They were sensuous reflections on life's intriguing possibilities—and losses.

He was best known around the world for ballads by Ellington or Billy Strayhorn that he totally possessed—"Warm Valley," "Day Dream," "I Got It Bad and That Ain't Good," and the "Come Sunday" section of "Black, Brown and Beige."

Hodges would rise from the reed section and, expressionless, gently move the dancers into heightened expectations of each other. When I was young, there were couples who played Ravel's *Bolero* as they joined behind closed doors in the early hours; but in my set, Johnny Hodges was on the record player sustaining intimacy though he and Duke were continents away.

Hodges played with more self-assurance than almost any musician I've ever seen. One exception was Charlie Parker, who became his horn—even when he looked as if he wasn't sure what city he was in. Another was Sidney Bechet, the moon-faced soprano saxophonist from New Orleans, who was an early mentor of Johnny Hodges. Bechet, too, possessed his instrument. Hodges's saxophone, on the other hand, seemed to play itself, with Hodges barely looking on.

His imperturbability could be startling. Once, in Boston years ago, I was standing in front of the bandstand when suddenly, behind me, screams erupted. I turned around to see that the dancers had, in panic, left a large open space in which two young men, each holding a knife, were circling each other.

The band played on with most of the players anxiously peering to see what was happening. Hodges, in the front row, had a clear view. He never took his eyes off the possibly homicidal ballet before him, but there was no indication at all of what if anything he felt. And, of course, he didn't miss a note.

Hodges left Ellington from 1951 to 1955 to lead a combo of his own. Renowned sidemen often did that, eagerly anticipating the leader's share of the money. Hodges also felt he had a particular grievance against Ellington. At rehearsals and record dates, Hodges, with his abundant melodic imagination, would "give" Ellington ideas that later appeared, he contended, in Ellington songs. Stanley Dance, the premier Ellington historian, has noted, "As the years passed, Hodges saw some of his ideas turn into

money-making hits by Ellington" and felt he had not been suffi-
ciently rewarded. Sometimes, after taking a solo on one of those
hits, Hodges would turn to Duke "while on stage and mimic
counting money, in full view of the audience." I saw him do that a
number of times. His face remained expressionless.

Hodges found that being a leader did not invariably provide
more income that one could keep, and there were far more wor-
ries than a sideman ever knew. So Hodges rejoined Ellington. But
while he was on his own, he made a series of memorable recordings for Norman Granz's Verve and Norgran labels.

The most careful of all jazz-reissue labels, Mosaic, has released
a boxed, six-LP set, *The Complete Johnny Hodges Sessions 1951–1955*
(Mosaic Records, 35 Melrose Place, Stamford, CT 06804). There
are notes by Stanley Dance, complete discographical information,
and a rare (cover) photograph of Johnny Hodges in which he
actually seems to be thinking of maybe smiling.

Among the other players is Lawrence Brown, the longtime
Ellington trombonist, who was capable of solos as intimately lyrical as those of Hodges but who also could play in a lusty, swash-
buckling manner that belied his own chronically serious
demeanor on the stand. Also present are the greatly underrated
trumpet players Emmett Berry and Harold "Shorty" Baker. The
hugely lyrical tenor saxophonist, Ben Webster, plays on some
sides, as does young John Coltrane who—after he had become the
new jazz prophet some years later—said of his former leader, "He
still kills me!"

Johnny Hodges died in 1970 at the age of sixty-two—not an
old man, in years or in his music. To the end, he played what
some musicians call "deep notes." Deeply, serenely erotic notes.

THE DUKE'S MEN

When he allowed himself substantial solo space, the orchestra leader proved to be a strikingly original pianist—with roots in the Harlem stride tradition and soundings beyond the horizon that were to influence Thelonious Monk. But most of the time, as both critics and musicians said in chorus, Duke Ellington's instrument was his orchestra.

He hired compellingly personal improvisers and then placed their singular voices in orchestral textures that both complemented them and made them serve *his* moods, fantasies, and memories.

Some of these fabled sidemen chafed at being so closely identified with this royal leader, and they left to make their own fame and fortune. It didn't work out. When Cootie Williams and Johnny Hodges, for instance, formed their own groups, they lacked the full flavor and authority that characterized their performances with Ellington. Although they were now in charge, they had become diminished.

But there had been a way for them to lead their own units— and take more solo space—without losing their moorings. During the 1930s, a series of recordings were made under the leadership of various Ellington sidemen—Williams, Hodges, Rex Stewart, and Barney Bigard. A sideman on nearly all the sessions was pianist Duke Ellington. Being congenitally incapable of being only a sideman, he helped shape the music. While some of the players were occasionally at odds with him about salary and other labor-management matters, they greatly respected his uncanny musicianship. They knew they had joined up—on the road and in recording studios—for a continuous master class.

These sessions of chamber jazz weren't just jam sessions. Enveloping moods were often created: the mysterious "Dooji Wooji"; a "Mobile Blues" that conjures up uncountable losses; the wry, relaxed "Tea and Trumpets"; and the majestically soaring "Jeep's Blues," which became a hit on jukeboxes all over Harlem.

There are many more pleasures and subtle surprises in two Columbia/Legacy sets, each containing two CDs: *The Duke's Men: Small Groups, Volume 1* and *Volume 2, 1934–1938*.

Alto and soprano saxophonist Johnny Hodges, who looked as if he were figuring out his tax returns on the bandstand, had a sound and ways of phrasing that went beyond romanticism to sensuous intimacy. Similarly, Lawrence Brown surpassed all other trombonists in his seemingly effortless lyricism that often referred most delicately to what goes on behind closed doors.

Cootie Williams was more than a "growl" trumpet player— although he was a distinctive successor to Bubber Miley in that specialty. Williams had an irresistible drive and sheer delight in plumbing the powers of his horn. Rex Stewart, a pungently urbane conversationalist on and off his horn—and an illuminating jazz historian—came close to talking on his instrument. His was a witty, ebullient style unlike that of any other jazzman.

Barney Bigard played a liquid clarinet in the New Orleans tradition, but with further dimensions of tone and jazz time absorbed in his travels through various jazz territories. Harry Carney, the large and imperturbably amiable baritone saxophonist who anchored the reed section, has been insufficiently appreciated for his ability to take his bulky instrument and somehow transform it, at times, into an appealingly gentle voice (as in "Blue Reverie" in this collection).

There are some clinkers in the sets, most notably the presence on a number of songs of one Mary McHugh. Helen Oakley Dance—who supervised many of these sessions and wrote the current notes—explains that McHugh, who sang with all the passion and dynamics of Justice William Rehnquist, was imposed on Ellington by Irving Mills. He thought the presence of a singer would increase the possibility of a jukebox hit.

Mills was Ellington's manager and publisher at the time, and his name appears as cocomposer on some of Ellington's perennial standards. Since Mills was not otherwise known as an accomplished or even journeyman composer or lyricist, the nature of his musical assistance to Ellington's work remains a mystery. Helen Dance reports that "Mills maintained that ideas contributed by him to a number of Duke's finished products entitled him to these credits." She does not, however, say what any of those ideas might have been.

Anyway, McHugh's presence turned out to be so wholly out of place that, Dance wrote, "When the session concluded, I commiserated with the group over the time wasted here. To my surprise, Johnny [Hodges] demurred. 'She's kind of cute,' he said." So who knows what makes for inspiration?

THE SWEETHEARTS OF RHYTHM

They were mighty engines, the big bands, barreling through the night like brightly lit trains, their whistles syncopating with the wheels on the tracks. They played small towns as well as the big-city movie houses. They hardly ever got off the road, because they were in such demand. By the dancers. But not only by the dancers.

While they lasted, the best-known—now legendary—illuminators of the night were Duke Ellington, Count Basie, Benny Goodman, Fletcher Henderson, Woody Herman, Jimmie Lunceford, and Charlie Barnet.

One band that should have been much more celebrated was composed entirely of women.

In the 1940s, Woody Herman hired a female trumpet player, Billie Rogers, thereby astonishing the jazz world. Women were part of the scene as singers and pianists, but everyone knew that a distaff horn player didn't have the physical strength to swing hard. Or the temperament. Chicks were too soft to roar and shout. Furthermore, a woman playing a horn (or drums or bass, for that matter) didn't look right. It was unfeminine. It was almost un-American.

Some of my high school buddies and I, giggling and slapping

our thighs, went to see the Woody Herman band and its freak show when it came to Boston, and we were shaking our heads in astonishment for days afterward. That chick had stood up with those guys in the brass section—and she had stood up *to* them. She had a big, crisp sound, and she sure could swing. There was no question about it. Billie Rogers was a woman all right, a jazz woman.

Gradually, other women horn players have, with some difficulty, established themselves in jazz—trombonist-arranger Melba Liston, for example, and the continually inventive soprano saxophonist Jane Ira Bloom. But many of the aficionados are still doubtful that women, unless they sing, belong in the front line. And the notion that there could be an all-female big band alongside bands made up of good old boys is considered ludicrous.

Well, there was such a band: The International Sweethearts of Rhythm. From 1937 to 1948 they proved that both collectively and in its hard-driving soloists, an all-female band could be a blazingly hot jazz force. Nonetheless, the Sweethearts are largely unknown to jazz buffs, except to some black listeners in their middle and later years and black musicians who were on the road at the same time as the Sweethearts.

The Sweethearts played mainly for black audiences, did not make many records, and were passed over for those Hollywood musicals that featured bands. They did make some short films, but those were not shown in white theaters. They were also seldom mentioned in the jazz magazines of the period. This was not because the band was predominantly black. After all, Count Basie and Duke Ellington were not overlooked. The jazz journalists of the time, almost entirely male, looked past the Sweethearts because they found it impossible to take a gaggle of young women seriously as jazz musicians.

At last, the first complete album by the International Sweethearts of Rhythm has been released—along with pictures and extensive historical notes. The woman responsible is Rosetta Reitz, who runs Rosetta Records, which is becoming justly renowned for its Women's Heritage Series—such reissues of blues and jazz rarities as "Mean Mothers" (International Women's Blues), "Women's Railroad Blues," and Ida Cox's "Wild Women Don't Have the Blues." The latter is in the Foremothers series. You get the picture.

There would have been no International Sweethearts of Rhythm if the head of the Piney Woods Country Life School in the Mississippi Delta—Laurence C. Jones—had not become aware of the profitable existence of two all-white female bands, Ina Ray Hutton's and Phil Spitalny's. This Mississippi school for poor and orphaned children was in chronic need of money, and it occurred to the headmaster that if he organized an all-girl band among his students, it would do better on the road than the groups of singers he'd been sending out for years.

The adjective *International* made sense because the band had Chinese and Indian saxophonists and a Hawaiian trumpeter. Later, some white young women also joined the Sweethearts, and when the band played the South, they had to wear dusty pancake. But there was occasional trouble with southern police anyway. As a black band member says in Linda Dahl's *Stormy Weather* (Pantheon), a history of jazz women, "We couldn't paint their eyes."

The Sweethearts became more and more professional until, by 1941, they were ready for the second most demanding jazz audience in the land—the audience at Harlem's Apollo Theater. The Sweethearts were asked back many times. Apollo patrons were the most demanding because they became part of the music. So were the dancers at the Savoy Ballroom in Harlem. The Sweethearts clicked there too.

By the mid-1940s—when the music in this set was first recorded, mainly from radio broadcasts—the Sweethearts were exhilaratingly in command of their powers. Among the swaggering soloists were Vi Burnside, a bristling, big-tone tenor saxophonist; Tiny Davis, an incisive hot trumpeter; and Anna Mae Winburn, a singer who sounded like a horn except that most horns couldn't phrase as insinuatingly as she did.

The Sweethearts stayed together longer than any distaff jazz band, and as Rosetta Reitz points out, they had a distinctive spirit, born of its members having been twice orphaned. On the road, the young women had only one another. The bus was their home because at many stops, restaurants and hotels were closed to them. And so they came closer together. Most of all, they wanted to show that, isolated though they were, they had the stuff to make the jazz big leagues.

By 1947, a number of the key players had left to form their own groups, and the Sweethearts came apart two years later. An attempt to revive the band ended in 1954. All that was left were a few rare recordings and the memories of those who had heard the Sweethearts.

When I used to hear tales of the music created by these traveling ladies, I figured they couldn't have been that good. But *International Sweethearts of Rhythm* (Rosetta RR 1312) reveals that they were better than their legend. So how come they're not even mentioned in "definitive" histories of big-band jazz? Maybe because even today few people believe that women could do such things.

PART II
"music all night—
and all day long"

KANSAS CITY: WALKING IN TIME

Count Basie's longtime drummer, Jo Jones ("the man who plays like the wind"), once tried to explain to me what it was about Kansas City in the 1930s that created a unique kind of swinging. It was more subtle and yet more irresistible than the jazz pulse in any other city.

Kansas City was a wide-open town, Jo Jones said, and so there was music all night—and all day long. Jazz so filled and moved the air that as people would go from one club to another, at noon or at midnight, "They'd be walking in time."

The paradigm of that Kansas City natural beat—as natural as breathing and walking—was Count Basie, as both a pianist and a leader of a band that made listeners feel like they were floating in time, even on ordinary nights.

Basie's credo was the jazz equivalent of "less is more." Over the years, his own playing became so spare that at times it might have seemed that the band could have done quite nicely without him. But when Basie was ill and another pianist filled in, the orchestra turned into a bunch of skilled civil servants. His notes were few, but each was precisely placed to keep the rhythm wave in the groove.

And, as his indispensable guitarist, Freddie Green, said:

"Listen to the way he makes different preparations for each soloist and the way, at the end of one of his own solos, he prepares an entrance for the next man. He leaves the way open."

Basie was not a showman like Duke Ellington and Earl Hines were in their different ways. He just sat at the piano, with a half-smile and an occasional nod. And with a single note, here and there, he effortlessly made a collection of proud individualists into a supple, often luminous whole. According to Basie, it was all as easy as it looked. When critics asked him what his grand artistic goal was, the answer was always the same: "I like to do things where you can halfway pat your feet."

But what, sir, are the principal aesthetic foundations of your art?

"The blues," he'd say. "We play a lot of blues. To me the blues is the start of an awful lot of things."

There were jazz writers who grumbled that Basie wasn't much of an interview. But he didn't see why all those questions were necessary when the music was so clear.

Over the years there has been a continuing festival of Basie reissues, abounding in solos and ensemble adventures that are as fresh, as clear, and as joyously swinging as when they were made. Columbia's *The Essential Count Basie* is true to its title. There are small-combo and big-band dates from 1936 to 1939, and the latter exemplify what Basie had in mind when he expanded his Reno Club (Kansas City) combo to a New York–based big band: "I wanted my fifteen-piece band to work together just like those nine pieces did. I wanted those four trumpets and three trombones to bite with real guts, but I wanted that bite to be just as tasty and subtle as if it were the three brass I used to use."

Among the classic epiphanies of the Basie credo in the Columbia set are "Goin' to Chicago Blues" (with Jimmy Rushing), "Rock-a-Bye Basie," "Miss Thing" (a two-part illumination of the lyrical art of dynamics), and the buoyant "Pound Cake." On this and most of the others, a ceaselessly intriguing soloist—the most abundantly and gently inventive in all of jazz history—was tenor saxophonist Lester Young. There were other wondrously distinctive players in the band (Buck Clayton, Dicky Wells, et al.), but Young, from the first note of his solo, compelled total attention.

While Columbia merits a hosanna for its Jazz Masterpieces

series, its history, like that of all the major labels, has been uneven with regard to jazz. During the sixties and much of the seventies, rock music pushed jazz to the outskirts of town. Count Basie, for one, would have seldom been able to record in those years had it not been for Norman Granz, who operated his Pablo Record label for himself and future generations and not particularly for contemporary sales.

Mr. Granz, a blunt, honest man with deeply abiding affection for what he regards as honest jazz, recorded many Basie albums (along with sets by Duke Ellington, Dizzy Gillespie, Roy Eldridge, and others for whom the big labels had no room). Pablo sets have become part of the Fantasy Records catalog, and some newly issued Basies have emerged.

One LP, *Fancy Pants*, is by a 1983 Basie band. The later Basie phalanxes were more aggressive than the quick and witty Basie band of the thirties, and the soloists were not as imaginative. Yet these were deeply swinging outfits that also reflected Basie's characteristic concern, and fun, with dynamics. Also, as various lightning bolts were cast during a number, there was the sense of a storm about to break—and sometimes it did.

Other Fantasy releases from the Granz vaults are two "walking in time" small-combo sessions: *The Count Basie Kansas City Septet* and *Count Basie Get Together*. Playing on both is a Basie veteran, the late Eddie "Lockjaw" Davis, who was one of the last of the tenor sax players with a sound so big it required no amplification in a club—or most other places. He also made each of his notes strut.

Trumpeter Snookie Young, who makes his horn speak rather than just play notes, is on the Kansas City date. On *Get Together*, the one-of-a-kind horns include trumpeters Harry "Sweets" Edison and Clark Terry and tenor Budd Johnson.

Throughout, on the combo and on the big-band dates, Count Basie is the keeper of the jazz time—the most powerfully unobtrusive figure the music has ever known.

MR. JONATHAN DAVID SAMUEL JONES

For every three beats a drummer plays, he owes Jo five.

—Max Roach

I realize that personally, myself, I'm fifty people.

—Jo Jones, in *The World of Count Basie*, by Stanley Dance

Yes, I dreamed last night
I was standing on 18th and Vine
Yes, I dreamed last night
I was standing on 18th and Vine
Well, I shook hands with Piney Brown
Well, I just couldn't keep from crying. . . .
Man, I got tears roll down from my eye
I like to hear my boys playing the blues all night long
It's 5 o'clock in the morning near the break of dawn
It sounds so mellow and nice
Man, it makes you think twice
'Cause that's where the world started
Everything's going to be all right. . . .

—"Piney Brown Blues"

Piney Brown, who ran a bar, was the big brother of us. No performer, small or large, ever came into Kansas City but what Piney Brown was willing to help him. But you had to be yourself. He didn't like any phonies.

—Jo Jones

A large number of friends of Jo Jones—all of whom had, in one way or another, been shaped by him—filled Saint Peter's Church on Lexington Avenue on Monday evening, September 9, 1985. John Garcia Gensel, the church's associate pastor, was the minister to the jazz community.

For hours that night, stories were told about Jonathan David Samuel Jones, gone at seventy-three. In front of the altar, Jo was there, in his coffin. And, for a while, he was there on a screen as Dave Chertok shared some choruses from his collection of jazz people on film.

As we watched the screen, we could not avoid Jo's eyes. They went through you, a musician was heard to say that night, like an X ray. Quick, quicker than sound, those eyes, catching all the things going on in the band at once—and among the dancers, too. When the music was floating—levitated by Basie, Freddie Green, Walter Page, and Jo—his eyes lit up the room, like when the world started. But if someone in a section wasn't taking care of business, he might have turned to stone if he had looked at Jo, who, sure as hell, was looking at him.

Jo Jones was the most ceaselessly alert man I have ever known. Off the stand, too. He was always, especially, on the lookout for his "kiddies"—the younger players Jo had picked out as worthy of his guidance. He taught them music and he taught them morality. To him, so far as jazz was concerned, the two were inextricably intertwined.

Anyone so remarkably fortunate as to be a jazz player, Jo believed, had been given an extraordinary privilege by God. "There shouldn't be any debauchery attached to it," he'd say. All the more so because debauchery distracted musicians from what they were here to do. And debauchery ultimately drained them of the spirit of the music.

A few nonmusicians also were selected by Jo to be his students of life. When I was nineteen, I had a jazz radio show in Boston and was a stringer for *Down Beat*. Jo decided that since I was going to be involved with the music, I'd better be instructed. At the Savoy Café one night, he sat me down until closing and told me where the music had come from, where he had come from, and how to listen. How to listen to what's really inside people, because that's what the music was about.

From then on, every once in a while, Jo would see me in a club or on the street and decide it was time for me to be administered another session of instruction, including whom to pay attention to among the players coming up. As he talked and I listened, his eyes would sweep the club or the street like a searchlight.

At Saint Peter's Church, at the funeral service, I told a story about Jo. In Kansas City, since the early 1920s, Baby Lovett had been a drummer beyond category. Count Basie once said of him, "There's a man that if a fly jumped down on a piece of paper, he'd play it." Baby Lovett was also a man who helped younger jazz musicians, some of them even before they could get themselves together enough to know they could use some help. And Baby was a delight to have on a session even before he got his drums set up.

Baby Lovett had been married for a long, long time, and when his wife died, he just about stopped functioning. He just sat at home and grieved. When Jo Jones heard what was happening, he canceled all his gigs for a month, flew to Kansas City, moved in with Baby Lovett, and, after a time, brought him back to life.

I was sitting with Jo one afternoon in a screening room, after we'd seen Bruce Ricker's invaluable movie about Kansas City jazz, *The Last of the Blue Devils*. Baby Lovett is in the film, playing with a grace and wit that calls Jo Jones to mind. I asked Jo about that month he'd taken off to be with Baby. In his raspy, staccato voice, Jo said there was nothing at all unusual about that. Anybody who thought there was just didn't know what the music is about.

Max Roach was one of the young players Jo Jones would look after to make sure they didn't lose their way. Jo, for instance, would stop in at the Apollo to see how the drummer for the International Sweethearts of Rhythm was doing, and then he'd go downtown, to all the downtowns with jazz in them. At the funeral service, Max Roach got up and said, "When I was on the road in those days, Jo was always popping up. I'd be in Kansas City or Chicago, and there he was in the audience. One night in Philadelphia, suddenly I saw him out there in the club.

"I played everything I could think of during that set. I hit everything I could hit. When the set was over, perspiring, I sat down next to Jo and waited. He knew how much I wanted to hear what he'd thought. Being Jo, he had to tell me what he thought—straight.

"Finally, Jo said, in that voice of his, 'All I could hear was your watch.'"

In the front row of the church, Roy Eldridge and Illinois Jacquet laughed. For all the notes you played, if you weren't saying anything, Jo wouldn't let you think that you were.

During a pause in the services, Eddie Locke and Roy Haynes, grand masters of jazz drumming, were talking. Locke had heard that sticks were in the coffin with Jo. He shook his head, "There should be some brushes in there." Jo, after all, used to be called the man who plays like the wind.

Roy Haynes reached into his suit pocket and took out a pair of brushes. "This is what I brought for him," he said.

Phil Schaap, a devoted jazz archivist, delivered the eulogy. He spoke of Jo's lessons in bandstand protocol: Do not let sadness or any complaint show in how you present yourself on the stand. That's not what people have come to see. Schaap might have added that the underside of that was: If you're hurting, you won't be able to keep that out of the music anyway.

And Schaap recalled the crispness and pride with which Jo made his way in the avenues of the world. His "blue jacket, blue tie with red stripe, gray pants, attaché case." Every time I have seen Jo, at all hours, he would not have had to change if he were suddenly summoned to address the United Nations.

It was all of a piece. If you were proud of what you were doing, you ought to look like you were. And there was no reason why a man of joy should not be well dressed. And Jo was, above all else, a creator of joy. He kept monitoring his "kiddies" so that they would get to where *they* could add to the joy and keep being a proud part of it.

For Jo, one of the places it started was at a circus to which his aunt had taken him when he was a child. "I can still *feel* that bass drum," he said much of a lifetime later. And though the drums were his true calling, Jo had to feel the music go through him in as many ways as he could. He played piano, trumpet, vibes, organ, saxophone. And he was a dancer. Until the very end, watching his hands, his eyes, you knew he was a dancer. He could sing too. Folks say nobody ever sang "Blues Jumped a Rabbit" the way Jo did.

It was in Kansas City in the 1930s that Jo found the promised land. The music never stopped in Kansas City. Literally. "You could be sleeping one morning at six A.M.," Joe recalled, "and a traveling band would come into town for a few hours, and they would wake you up to make a session with them. You never knew what time in the morning someone would knock on the door and say they were jamming down the street."

And at work, "it wasn't unusual for one number to go on for about an hour or an hour and a half. Nobody got tired. They didn't tell me at the time that they used to change drummers [during the night], so I just sat there and played the whole time for pure joy."

As he spread the joy, Jo often took you unawares. One night in Boston, he left the drums, left the stand, and with just his hands tapping a chair started to take his listeners out of ordinary time.

Moving around the room, playing with his fingers or with the palms of his hands or his knuckles, he drew rhythms and melodies from tables, chairs, the floor, the walls, the very air. Grinning fiercely, Jo mesmerized his listeners for nearly an hour without going back to the bandstand. For them, straight time had stopped; they were in his time.

Just as suddenly as he had left the stand, Jo, looking as cool and crisp as when he had started, reappeared behind the drums, greatly resembling the Cheshire cat on the verge of disappearing again.

The last time I saw and heard Jo play was at the Kool Jazz Festival tribute to Count Basie at Carnegie Hall in June 1984. Friends and former Basie colleagues backstage were marveling that he was there at all, for he had been variously and sometimes very seriously ill in recent years.

"He just won't go," Basie alumnus Marshall Royal said. The others nodding, smiling.

In April 1984, Jo had had a stroke. And then pneumonia. Backstage at Carnegie Hall that night, he needed help to get around. And when he was sitting in a chair, waiting to go on, Jo, for once, wasn't saying much. But his eyes were talking. About playing.

When it was time, Jo, alone on stage, started slow and uncertain. But he was using both arms, even though the left arm had been hanging almost useless since his stroke. Then, his eyes shining, Jo got it together. The drums were talking now, and although he was supposed to have been on for only a few minutes, Jo wasn't about to leave.

In the wings, George Wein, who was producing the concert along with me, looked at his watch, frowning at the shadow of overtime. Jo, grinning, the joy rising in him, shouted fiercely at Wein, *"I'm not going back in there no more!"*

At last, rather than having Wein go out to pull him off, as Wein had intended, Joe Williams, leading a group of musicians, joined Jo out there. And once his family had gently shaped a final chorus for him, Jo had no choice but to go back into the wings, and into the night.

"I WASN'T BORN NO CHILD. I WAS BORN A MAN"

[When I was young], I saw a black woman in South Alabama out on roller skates all by herself on a rink where she didn't have no business being. She was wonderful, and I was watching her when this white man turned to me and said, "Do you know who that is?" I didn't. He said, "That's Miss Bessie Smith." Can you imagine that? A white man in Alabama calling a black woman Miss. I couldn't believe it. Bessie Smith, mister!

—Jo Jones, *Modern Drummer,* January 1984

Some years ago, I visited a predominantly black elementary school in Columbus, Ohio. I had been told it was a place where kids actually learned because they were expected to learn. From what I could tell in a few hours, the school deserved its reputation. At one point, the principal, a black woman in her late thirties, took me on a tour of the building. On the walls were portraits of distinguished black Americans—Ralph Bunche, Marian Anderson, Booker T. Washington, W. E. B. Du Bois, Roy Wilkins, and a good many more.

When the tour was over, I asked her if I'd missed the portraits of Duke Ellington, Louis Armstrong, or Count Basie. Were they in some other part of the building?

The principal pursed her lips and looked at me with searing scorn: "We do not put pictures of *entertainers* on our walls!"

In the early 1970s, I ran into Marian McPartland in a Washington television studio. She was in the city to orchestrate a tribute to Duke Ellington by a large contingent of children from the D.C. public schools. Marian was very pleased at how well the kids were getting into the music, but one thing saddened her.

"I asked the children," she told me, "how many of them knew who Duke Ellington was. Only a few did."

These days, with a Washington high school of the arts bearing his name, the kids who go to that school know who he was. But how many other students in the District of Columbia have the slightest idea that Ellington was the most abundantly original composer in the history of the country? And a composer who in his work—from "Black Beauty" and "Harlem Airshaft" to "Black, Brown and Beige"—wrote of the black experience in America, from its beginnings, with extraordinary depth, wit, tenderness, and strength. How many schoolkids of any color anywhere in the United States know anything about Ellington? Or Lester Young? Or Charles Mingus? Or Bessie Smith? Or Jo Jones? They have been deprived of the richest, most distinctive strain of their own cultural heritage. And most of them stay culturally deprived for the rest of their lives.

One young Dane, making his first visit to New York, said to me in astonishment, "You mean there is not a statue of Charlie Parker in Times Square?"

The day after Charlie Parker died, Art Blakey said to a reporter, "I wonder how many black kids knew who Bird was." Or white kids.

The jazz heritage is not only about music. Like Charlie Parker said, jazz comes from who you are, where you've been, what you've learned: "If you don't live it, it won't come out of your horn."

The players who were originals and became part of the sounds and cadences of those who followed can be studied as classic American heroes. In the tradition of heroes everywhere, they have transcended great odds—in this case, being black and on the road when Jim Crow was glaring out the windows of just about every American town and city, and not only in the South, by any means. In your own town, however, you knew what to expect; but traveling constantly, a black jazzman always ran the risk of being surprised by a local custom that could split his head open.

In a social studies class in the school in Columbus, the kids would have learned a lot about black resilience and ingenuity from Charles Mingus, Jo Jones, and Max Roach (all of whom would have been delighted to come when they had gigs in the area).

Jo Jones also might have talked about his father. It wasn't only jazz musicians who knew how to survive without bending. In January 1973, during an interview with Milt Hinton for an Institute of Jazz Studies-Smithsonian Institution oral-history project, Jo spoke of his father.

"He was connected with the government," said Jo. "He was what is known as an artificer—along with being an electrician—building boats and things. And you must remember the social conditions at that particular time. It was very difficult to find an outlet for him, but due to his flair and due to what he knew, his services were requested in different places, and he had to go wherever that was. What made it particularly difficult was for him, as a black man, to come into an area that he was not supposed to come into. He also had to be four times better than anybody else to get what he did.

"My father was the type of person, when they had the diving suits, he didn't use a diving suit. He could go underwater and stay three minutes without breathing. It was phenomenal. He would just go right under the water, go in, and fix up whatever had happened. He was the only one of his kind."

When Jo Jones was eleven, his father was killed in an accident as he was trying to help a number of black college students fix some machinery on a barge where they were working during the summer. A piece of steel plunged into his back.

So Jo grew up early. Many years later, in the manner of a warrior speaking in an epic tale, Jo said to writer Chip Stern: "I wasn't born no child. I was born a man. Not a baby. Not a boy. A man, in capital letters. No questions, no semicolons, no parentheses, no commas. Period. A man!"

I've heard other family stories from jazz players that school-kids ought to hear. And then there are the stories of legendary jazz battles, fought not with broad swords or artillery, but with shining horns. Fought all night long and into the next day. During these jousts, kings were dethroned; and apprentice players, watching, dreamed of the time when they would dare to enter the lists against the dread champions of previous jam sessions.

In his interview with Milt Hinton, Jo Jones alluded to one of the most resounding of those battles, a war of the tenors in Kansas City. A full account is in the book *Hear Me Talkin' to Ya*. (That volume, in which the story of jazz up to 1955 was told entirely in the musicians' own words, was put together by Nat Shapiro and me thirty years ago. The musicians in it chronicle many confrontations and triumphs, ranging across decades and the whole country. So far as I know, not a single public school ever has used the book in a class.)

At the center of that tumultuous Kansas City night was Coleman Hawkins (Bean, as he was known, because he knew so much). He had invented the jazz tenor saxophone, and he had never been defeated at any of the "cutting sessions," as they were called, anywhere in the country. Like a fabled gunslinger for whom everyone would make more than ample room when he came into a bar, Hawkins would stride into a town and wait to be challenged. He never showed much outward emotion, but his eyes kind of gleamed in anticipation of the next slaughter of the innocents.

Actually, by that time—1934—not many young tenors were trying any longer to enter into combat with Hawkins. At many of the sessions they would just show him how much they'd learned, or thought they'd learned, since he'd rode into town the last time.

But this night, in Kansas City, there was thunder in the air when Hawkins came into the Cherry Blossom. Word immediately went out that the boss of all tenors was there, and within half an hour, bearing their horns, Lester Young, Herschel Evans, Ben Webster, and a few others strode into the club.

As Mary Lou Williams recalled, "Bean didn't know the Kaycee tenor men were so terrific, and he couldn't get himself together though he played into the morning. I happened to be nodding that night, and around four A.M., I awoke to hear someone pecking on my screen.

"I opened the window on Ben Webster. He was saying, 'Get up, pussy cat, we're jammin' and all the pianists are tired out now. Hawkins has got his shirt off, and he's still blowing. You got to come down.' "

Mary Lou came down, and it was true. Bean was being banged against the ropes. But he wouldn't give up. He kept trying to defeat his adversaries with some kind of new idea until it was light. And he kept trying past the dawn. Finally, knowing that he had to be in Saint Louis that night for a gig with the band he worked for, Fletcher Henderson's, Bean gave up. He leapt into his new Cadillac, and by the time he had pushed it as hard as he could to St. Louis, he had burned out the car.

Not that tenors elsewhere became eager to tangle with Hawkins once the word got out. Long, long afterward, the attitude toward Bean by kids coming up was distilled in this conversation between a young player and a jazz veteran:

"Coleman Hawkins scares me, man."

"He's supposed to scare you," the older musician said.

In all of these cutting sessions, the most acclaimed classical virtuoso would have been left for dead in twelve seconds. Without score paper in front of him, what would he have had of his own to say? And even if he could have thought of something to say, not being an improviser, he wouldn't have known how to say it. So who are the more creative artists—classical or jazz musicians?

In his notes for the Time-Life *Coleman Hawkins* set, John McDonough tells how this enormously independent, proud musician—who always kept hearing into the future—handled his last battle. In 1969, ailing, Hawkins had insisted on keeping all his commitments, and one day in May a colleague came by to pick Bean up for a gig.

"He knocked on his door and waited. He heard sounds inside, but no answer. After a few minutes he called a security guard, who came up and opened the door. Inside they found Hawkins with his hat and coat on, unable to stand but crawling across the living room floor toward the door, dragging his horn behind him."

At the funeral, Russell Procope said, "He had a presence, even lying there in the casket. I looked at his hands where they were folded together, and I thought of how much they had achieved."

Looking into the caskets of Jo Jones, Duke Ellington, Charlie Parker, and other jazz makers, I've thought the same. And I've thought about how many Americans don't even know their names.

But those classic American heroes who have gone sure knew they were here. "For all the pain and problems we endured being black men in America," Jo Jones said, "we really had some wonderful times."

THE CHIEF WOULD BE PROUD

In the 1950s, if you walked down the stairs to the cellar that was Birdland, there were nights when the sound came up at you and almost bounced you against the wall, it was so powerful and palpable. Those were the nights the Count Basie band was on the stand. It wasn't the floating, subtly unpredictable band of instrumental dancers that Basie had brought east from Kansas City in the mid-1930s, but the later version, with its crisp swing and robust soloists, was exhilaratingly satisfying too.

No one enjoyed the band more than Basie himself. So much so that toward the end, when he became ill and needed wheels to get to the piano, he stayed on the road. "If I wasn't having a good time, I wouldn't be out here," he'd say when asked why he didn't cool it at home.

The Count—or the Chief, as his men called him—died in 1984, but the band kept on. That's what the Chief had wanted. Guitarist Freddie Green, who had been a Basie sideman for half a century, noted that Basie had let it be known that the tradition must continue so long as people wanted to come and listen. And tenor saxophonist Eric Dixon added, "I can tell you after twenty-four years here that this band plays by itself. No matter who you put in front of it, it plays Basie. He put the spirit into it."

Nonetheless, somebody has to be put in front of a band. And as of 1983, the right leader was chosen both to keep the founder's spirit going and to extend it, on occasion, to forms and colors that

Basie himself might have been wary of. He is Frank Foster, a tenor saxophonist who used to play and arrange for Basie. Accustomed to command, he directed a number of his own groups through the years, among them a big band called the Loud Minority.

Listening to the Basie band at the Blue Note in New York, I was delighted once again to be in the teeth of the gale that used to hit me walking down into Birdland. Like the best of the Basie orchestras during the past thirty years, this one combines bristling precision with a deeply flowing groove. As Quincy Jones said to me a while ago, "No synthesizer, no matter how advanced, can make you feel as good as a big jazz band."

The arrangements are still uncluttered, and the musicians clearly enjoy being able to play music rather than thickets of notes. Despite his conducting, announcing, and programming responsibilities, Mr. Foster solos almost as often as he would have sitting in the reed section years ago. He loves to play and doesn't see why he should be deprived, particularly since he's in charge. The Chief also enjoyed playing, but in a wily, very spare style in which one note, at exactly the right moment, propelled the band more powerfully than a score of drummers could have. Pianist Tee Carson comes very close to approximating the catalytic Basie touch. A veteran of the road, Mr. Carson has the knowing air of a pianist in an old Dodge City saloon.

The tunes range through the Basie book—Neal Hefti's "Li'l Darlin'," the Basie-Green "Corner Pocket," the new leader's classic "Shiny Stockings," and a strutting Eric Dixon arrangement from the Ellington book, "Things Ain't What They Used to Be." In that one, as climaxes build on climaxes, the trombone section rises as one with a shout that fills the Blue Note and sweeps through the doors into Greenwich Village. So much for synthesizers.

The keeper of the Basie spirit, Mr. Foster is, like the Chief, hard to anger. But he does get crusty when someone puts the orchestra into the category of "ghost bands," those dim ensembles that crisscross the country under the name of departed leaders, playing the arrangements of the original crews, often with a rather eerie air of unreality.

"Damn it," says Mr. Foster, "this ain't no 'ghost band'!" An overwhelmingly live band is precisely what Basie had in mind so that, like Joe Hill, it could be said of him that he never quite left the scene.

PART III
the human instrument

WHAT MAKES A JAZZ SINGER?

The quickest way to start a long argument among jazz musicians and aficionados is to ask them to make up a list of certified jazz singers. Not jazz-influenced vocalists, but the real swinging thing. Louis Armstrong would make every list, because his trumpet playing and his singing were indivisible. One flowed right into the other without a break.

The jazz credentials of Billie Holiday are also beyond argument. To instrumentalists, playing with Lady Day was like jamming after hours among themselves. She moved inside a song the way they did. And as I can attest, Billie could simply say hello, and the sound and rhythm of that one word became the very definition of jazz.

Both Billie and Louis are part of *The Jazz Singers* (Prestige), a two-LP array of twenty-three vocalists from the classical age (Bessie Smith) to the present (Sarah Vaughan). The set is valuable both for pleasure, which is what jazz is about, and as a vivid aid in finding out for yourself what the indispensable elements of jazz singing actually are.

It is not enough, for instance, to imitate a jazz horn—as happens a few times every long night in motel bars around the country when singers pretend to be antic alto saxophones or jittery trombones. The true jazz singer does not try to be a horn, but rather to phrase and glide and swing with the suppleness of a horn while not distorting or rushing or mashing the lyrics. It is the art of being a hornlike singer rather than an artificial horn.

Mildred Bailey, for instance, in "Rockin' Chair" in this collection, is a sly marvel of graceful, witty surprises as she plays with both the melodic line and the beat to transform this standard utterly. She could not have improvised with so much fun and assurance had she not heard thousands of hours of jazz horn playing behind her, but she absorbed the flowing grammar of all those horns without herself turning into metal.

Among other distillations of this demanding art in *The Jazz Singers* is Jimmy Rushing's "I Left My Baby (Standing in the Backdoor Crying)" with the Count Basie All-Stars. Rushing—a large man of extraordinary poise and a wide range of moods, from rambunctious exuberance to poignancy that is almost unbearable, as here—was one of the most urbane of jazz singers. Were there a jazz Mozart, Rushing would have been his Don Giovanni. In his way, quite different from Billie Holiday's or Mildred Bailey's, he too had so mastered time that everything he sang had a deeply relaxed, swinging pulse. Indeed, the silences between the notes swung just as deeply.

Rushing, Bailey, Holiday, and Armstrong never sang anything but jazz, no matter what the song was. Some performers, however, try to move between jazz and pop, and if they take that ferry too often, their jazz singing becomes suspect. Joe Williams, for instance, dismally anticlimaxed a Carnegie Hall evening devoted to him during the 1983 Kool Jazz Festival with an "inspirational" pop medley that would have been far more appropriate for his Las Vegas appearances or a Pat Boone barbecue. Leaving the hall, some jazz die-hards were muttering that Williams never really was a jazz singer anyway—just an entertainer who had happened to luck onto a long-term association with Count Basie that gave him jazz status.

Well, depending on the night you hear him, Williams can be an unforgettable jazz singer, as in "Goin' to Chicago Blues" in this set. Recorded in a nightclub—Williams should stay out of recording studios because they stiffen him—this is a brilliant, risky, seven-minute demonstration of the incandescent essence of jazz singing.

With prowling wit, he so firmly controls the beat that he can break it, turn it inside out, play it like a yo-yo, put it all back together, and then, a second later, surprise you all over again.

Being an intimate of time—being able to play with it continually without losing it—is indispensable to jazz singing. This can be heard in Dinah Washington's rendition of "I've Got a Feeling I'm Falling" and Fats Waller's "There'll Be Some Changes Made."

One of the subtlest masterpieces of jazz timing—as well as jazz storytelling—is "I Got It Bad and That Ain't Good" with Ivie Anderson and Duke Ellington's orchestra. Anderson, not nearly so well known as she ought to be, was a singer who never overstated a note. She could suggest more in a phrase than many singers were able to in several choruses. Jazz singing, then, is also knowing what to leave out.

As Ed Michel, the producer of this album, says in the notes, he couldn't include all the jazz singers in this cornucopia, but I wish he had found room for Betty Carter, the most beguilingly unpredictable jazz vocalist now performing. Her ways with time can be dizzying, for she keeps so many rhythms, explicit and implicit, in the air that when the song is over, it's a wrench to have to adjust yourself to just plain ordinary time.

I would also have included Bing Crosby, for I am among that select minority for whom Bing is a joyfully authentic jazz singer. But not Frank Sinatra. Bing was much more of an improviser than Sinatra. He could swing with much more ease, and he phrased in a way that reminded you that he used to room with Bix Beiderbecke. Sinatra has certainly been shaped by jazz (he acknowledges the influence of Billie Holiday). But if you threw him in with a bunch of improvising hornmen—without arrangements and without a conductor—Frank might have to be rescued very quickly. Bing, however, could be all by himself on a country road and work up a pretty fair series of swinging jazz choruses without a bit of strain.

There are times, of course, when there are no doubts at all about who can sing jazz and who can't. I remember hearing Dizzy Gillespie and Max Roach accompanying a singer in "Salt Peanuts" on the White House lawn. He sure was earnest, that singer, but he and time just didn't get along. His name was Jimmy Carter.

THE LAST YEARS OF LADY DAY

She didn't sing many blues, but Billie Holiday often had them. Backstage, in her autumnal years, she'd sometimes growl, "The only reason they're out there is to see me fall into the damn orchestra pit." She was right about some in the audience. During that decade, the 1950s, Billie was said to be on the way down and out. So, as in the final years of Charlie Parker, there were those who paid money in hope of seeing a legend fall apart before their very eyes.

Indeed, there were nights when Billie, weary or high or both, could barely be heard, which was just as well. But there were other times when she sang with such depth of feeling and intelligence that by contrast, her airy 1930s recordings, while still utterly charming, sounded like the romantic illusions of a young woman. Billie had learned a lot since then, whether she'd wanted to or not.

A year before she died, I was talking about Billie with Miles Davis, who has much harsher standards of jazz performance than any critic. Davis was commenting, with his customary expletives, on the notion that Holiday was in a state of precipitous decline. First of all, he said, her voice had become deeper and darker, which was right for what she now wanted to say. "You know, she's not thinking now what she was in nineteen thirty-seven."

Second, "She still has control, probably more control now than then."

Her control toward the end is intriguingly evident in a group of reissues of the Verve recordings she made for Norman Granz during the 1950s. No other label would have recorded her as often as Granz did in those years because her albums didn't sell that much. It was the time of bop and then cool jazz and soul jazz, while Billie's only category was herself.

Norman Granz, who grew up on jam sessions and still greatly prefers spontaneity to even the most elegant scores, gave Billie Holiday and her colleagues as much freedom as they wanted to take. Had she been as weak and musically insecure as she was supposed to be, Billie would have cushioned herself with arrangements and strings on these sessions. But on all of them she was out there in the bare studio, alongside a few strongly individualistic horns, and with a lot of space in which to move.

The reissues on the Verve label are *Embraceable You, Stormy Blues,* and *The History of the Real Billie Holiday.* There are two LPs in each album.

Among the singing horns accompanying Billie's hornlike phrasing and beat on these tracks are Harry "Sweets" Edison and Charlie Shavers, trumpets; Ben Webster, tenor saxophone; Benny Carter, alto saxophone; and often, on piano, Jimmy Rowles. It's clear, as they interact with the singer, why jazz musicians always enjoyed working with her. There was no singer who could swing as surely and subtly as she could—and with such wit, sometimes playful, sometimes desperate.

Listening to "When Your Lover Has Gone," "Just Friends," "Embraceable You," and "Nice Work If You Can Get It" affirms the judgment of Benny Green, a onetime British jazzman who has become an essayist on literary matters. He wrote that Billie Holiday's singing during the 1950s exposed "the true core of her art, her handling of a lyric." These last recordings by her, he added, are "not the insufferable croakings of a woman already half dead, but recitatives whose dramatic intensity becomes unbearable, statements as frank and tragic as anything throughout the whole range of popular art."

I can hear Billie, backstage, growling with a smile, "Why the hell didn't he write that when it could have done me some good?"

DOWN TO STEAMBOAT TENNESSEE

Her look was that of a lady of exceptional, refined independence. Not a snob by any means, but at first rather distant, Lee Wiley was what later came to be called laid back. She was a small-town girl—from Fort Gibson, Oklahoma—but she hadn't been in New York too long before she was singing Cole Porter's songs as if he had written them about her. Yet her way with those songs, and everything else she tried, was unlike that of any jazz singer before or since.

Lee Wiley had influences, primarily Ethel Waters, but the cool sensuality of her sound and phrasing immediately *identified* her. She was a romantic, like such of her jazz pals as Bunny Berigan, but she also thought that excesses of any kind were funny, so there was often a gently mocking obbligato to her love songs. As for her jazz time, she was one of those improvisers who didn't have to even think about swinging. The pulse, the flow, and the flexibility of her beat were as natural a part of her as the discreetly erotic vibrato that, in certain wordless passages, promised initiation into incomparable rites.

Her best recordings included two sets made in 1939 and 1940 by a label owned by the Liberty Music Shop in New York. The shop was a place for the carriage trade. There were no discounts on recordings or anything else. And the store's record label had been devoted primarily to the kinds of performers most likely to appeal to fun-loving folks on Park Avenue: Beatrice Lillie, Ethel Merman, Cy Walter, and various sparkling interpreters of moderately rare show tunes.

The proprietor of Liberty Music Shop was somewhat apprehensive at giving over an album to jazz transients, but the customers very much approved. And Cole Porter's reaction to the side containing his music was: "I can't tell you how much I like the way she sings these songs."

Listening again, as I often have since 1939, to Lee Wiley adding her own knowing spirit to "Let's Fly Away," "You Do Something to Me," "Hot-House Rose," and "Easy to Love," I also hear in my head a 1971 radio interview with Lee Wiley, which could be subtitled "Only in America."

Part Cherokee, part Scottish, part English, she was born and grew up in a place she once described as "about as small as a town can get." It was clear early on that she was kind of different from the others there. She recalled: "I used to sit in school and dream about being a singer. In the back of the class, of course. And I had a boyfriend who would skip school with me, and we would go over to the local store and play records. The records that we listened to and liked were called 'race records.' And they were only sold in a certain part of the town, the colored part." (The records were by Ethel Waters and Bessie Smith.) Her mother strongly disapproved of those trips.

There are some things you have to do, no matter what your mama says. She split, as jazz players used to say, when she was fifteen, tested the waters in Saint Louis, Chicago, and New York, and for a while, in the 1930s, was a prime-time featured singer on "Kraft Music Hall" with Paul Whiteman. She continued in radio, played clubs, made records, never made a lot of money but always knocked out musicians and quite a few of us among the laity. Lee Wiley died in 1975. She was sixty-five.

The cover of the Liberty Music Shop Gershwin-Porter reissue shows young Lee Wiley, dressed in a formal but not too severe black jacket and white skirt, looking at you. Her look is appraising, slightly amused. She was always curious. For a while.

BING CROSBY: JAZZ SINGER

When I was a kid in Spokane," Bing Crosby once told me, "I played drums in a six-piece band. We couldn't read music, but we just about memorized all the new records by the Mound City Blues Blowers, the Memphis Five, and the Original Dixieland Jazz Band. Those sounds, those wonderful sounds, made me determined to somehow work my way into the company of jazz musicians. Salary didn't mean a thing to me in those years. I just wanted to be in that environment."

And so he was, as a member of the Rhythm Boys, who sang with Paul Whiteman from 1926 to 1930. His roommate on the road for a time was Bix Beiderbecke, long portrayed as the classic jazz legend—the young man with a horn who drank himself to death because he could not bear too much reality.

But "it wasn't booze that killed Bix," Crosby said. "He wasn't an alcoholic. He was a jolly absentminded sort of fellow, but he was so totally immersed in music that he never ate or slept properly. His health broke from exhaustion. Of course, it seemed that none of us went to bed in those days. It's amazing that some of us survived."

Starting in the early 1930s, Crosby left the full-time company of jazz musicians to star on radio and then in films. And he kept on recording, often with jazz improvisers in the band. Although

Crosby is most renowned as what used to be called a crooner—someone who transforms ballads into intimate conversations—he also, when the spirit moved him, sang jazz with buoyant authority.

He was not just a "jazz-influenced" singer. Crosby could be the real thing. For instance, on a Columbia Jazz Masterpiece album, *1930's: The Jazz Singers,* the one Crosby track—"Dinah," with the Mills Brothers—is a short course in the essentials of the jazz vocal. The instrumental phrasing; the hot scat singing over the flowing vocal rhythm section that was the Mills Brothers; and the last chorus, on which Bing sounds like a joyful, driving cornet.

In addition, Columbia assembled a three-LP (and CD) set, *Bing Crosby/The Crooner/The Columbia Years 1928–1934.* Not all the numbers, by any means, are jazz pieces, but even on the ballads there are touches of phrasing and rhythm that indicate Crosby was never without—in his head—the company of jazz musicians.

The collection includes the most startling of all Crosby recordings. "Brother Can You Spare a Dime?" is neither jazz nor pop music. Yip Harburg and Jay Gorney's song is a monologue by a veteran who, once cheered as a soldier, now is down and out. Behind Crosby, the orchestra plays a slow, relentless march, and he tells his story—from the breadline—with a chilling bitterness that is wholly at odds with the blithe Bing of the Kraft Music Hall, *Holiday Inn,* and *High Society.* Yet the serious Crosby, who knew something of failure and loss, emerged again later in his career when he played an alcoholic as if he had been one, in the film version of Clifford Odets's *The Country Girl.*

As for the light-hearted Crosby, still urbanely charming and musically beyond fashion, there is a remarkable store of rare Crosby radio broadcasts issued by Crosby aficionado Larry Kiner. On his Spokane label, for example, *Bing & Dinah* is composed largely of duets by Crosby and a Dinah Shore who used to be a pretty fair jazz singer herself on broadcasts by, as I remember, the Chamber Music Society of Lower Basin Street. Her delightful, genuinely relaxed rhythmic sense blends naturally with Crosby's.

On Bing's *Music Hall Highlights*—a selection from the Kraft Music Hall programs—Mr. Kiner has programmed a jazz performance featuring "After You've Gone" and such other songs that could have been written for Crosby as "It's Only a Paper Moon" and "Moonlight Bay." Among the other albums in the Spokane collection are *Bing and Connee Boswell, Bing & Bob Hope,* and a series of *Bing in the Thirties.*

Included on the Kraft Music Hall sets are some of the breezy Crosby spoken exchanges that used to add to the casual surprises of that program. I knew there were writers on the show, but listening then, some of the wordplay still seemed so singularly Crosby's that I figured he must have often ad-libbed. During a 1976 interview, he confirmed that he had, and I asked him about his pleasure in playing with words.

"Well," he said, "I read a lot. I'm no intellectual, you understand, but I like Graham Greene, Evelyn Waugh, Hemingway, John P. Marquand, Louis Auchincloss, and Simenon. There's a great writer! Simenon writes mystery stories, but he really understands character."

Politically, Crosby was a conservative; the *National Review* was one of his favorite publications. But unlike Bob Hope, John Wayne, and Jimmy Stewart, he never so publicly identified himself with a party's candidate that he appeared to be endorsing him. "I never thought it was proper," Crosby told me, "for a performer to use his influence to get anyone to vote one way or another."

There was, however, one political issue that he felt very strongly about, and he might have said so publicly but he couldn't figure out a way to make a difference. "I was against the Vietnam War," he said, "but I didn't know what to do about it."

I asked if there was anything he hadn't done in all those years that he still wanted to try. "No," Crosby said. "I really have accomplished just everything I wanted to. It's been a good life, pleasing people over so many years."

And the recordings continue to bring pleasure, for all through his career—as in *High Society,* with Louis Armstrong—Crosby still remembered that six-piece kid band in Spokane, with himself on drums. And he also remembered how—with Bix and other jazz luminaries—he habitually used to take in after-hours jam sessions in whatever cities the Paul Whiteman group played.

"Back then," Bing told me, "there was a color line almost anywhere else. But not at those sessions. You could hear Bix and Louis Armstrong and Willie "The Lion" Smith, all mixed together. The jazz scene was way ahead of the rest of the country."

A JAZZ BAND COMPOSED
ONLY OF SINGERS:
LAMBERT, HENDRICKS & ROSS

There were only three of them—Jon Hendricks, Dave Lambert, and the wittiest of all hipsters, Annie Ross—but in a club or concert hall there were nights when they sounded like a rambunctious big band. Neither before nor since has there been a jazz vocal group with so much infectious delight in its swinging vocation.

Unlike singing groups that used the lyrics of standard tunes as launch pads for improvisation, this trio's basic repertory consisted of putting lyrics to celebrated and not-so-celebrated jazz instrumental solos. For instance, Peanuts Holland's trumpet solo on Charlie Barnet's "Charleston Alley" or Ben Webster's roller-coaster tenor solo on Duke Ellington's recording of "Cottontail." The resident lyricist was Hendricks, whose years inside the jazz scene gave him an easy command of the spoken jazz idiom backstage and in bars.

For all the fun they obviously were having as they sang and scatted, the members of the trio tried to do justice to the instrumental inventions they were appropriating. The musicians whose horn solos had been transformed into vocal flights by Lambert, Hendricks & Ross listened to the changes with much proprietary interest.

Usually, they were not disappointed. Once, at the Newport Jazz Festival, trumpeter Buck Clayton said to Hendricks, "That solo of mine you sang on 'Goin' to Chicago' is the prettiest thing I ever heard in my life."

"Well, Buck," Hendricks replied, "I didn't do anything but put words to what you played."

Clayton looked at him. "Did I play all of that?"

On the other hand, there was the time Annie Ross vocalized a Miles Davis solo on "Now's the Time" in a way characterized by Hendricks as "fatuous" and "limp." Months later, Hendricks—as he recalled in an interview in the jazz magazine *Cadence*—was in a Toronto restaurant about to address a steak. Miles Davis walked in, sat down, pushed Hendricks aside, and ate the steak.

"Man," said the astounded and aggrieved Hendricks, "you ate my steak!"

"You mess with my solos," said Davis, "I mess with your food."

The audience for Lambert, Hendricks & Ross consisted of far more than musicians checking out the additions to their inventions. During its life—1957 to 1964 (Ross left in 1962)—the trio had an enthusiastic following here and abroad. A key element of its appeal was the scat-singing prowess of all three vocalists. This form of high-speed wordless improvisation requires instant imagination.

In Columbia's reissue of Lambert, Hendricks & Ross—*Everybody's Boppin'*, in its Jazz Masterpieces series—there is a particularly jubilant scat-singing duel between Lambert and Hendricks on the title track. But exultant scat singing abounds on most of the other cuts as well.

The sounds the group made on recordings could be so complex and multilayered that I was sure much of it was overdubbed until I first saw and heard Lambert, Hendricks & Ross in a club.

The foundation of these natural aural highs was the original, actual sounds of the horn solos they chose to illuminate. "I insisted," Hendricks told me recently, "that they try, with their voices, to get the timbre of the instrument that played the original solo." But the result went beyond imitation. In the ensemble passages and in the solos themselves, the irrepressible temperaments of the singers brought textures, flavors, and dynamics to the music that were the sole property of Lambert, Hendricks & Ross.

Dave Lambert, a gentle man, died in 1966, characteristically trying to help somebody. He saw a motorist struggling to change a tire, stopped to give a hand, and was hit by a passing car. Annie Ross, originally from England, moved back there for a while but later was based in Los Angeles. Although she still occasionally sings, she now works mostly at film acting. Included in this Columbia Lambert, Hendricks & Ross retrospective is one of Ross's abiding triumphs, "Twisted," based on Wardell Gray's tenor solo. Its message, as Dave Lambert used to say, is: "Anybody who goes to a psychiatrist ought to have his head examined."

Hendricks went on to become the precise director of a singing group, Jon Hendricks and Company.

"Each night we work," Hendricks says, "I say to the audience that we are dedicated to the perpetuation of the sound of Lambert, Hendricks & Ross, the greatest vocal group ever to perform on the planet Earth."

"After I say that," Hendricks laughs, "I wait for someone to contradict me. And it never happens."

CARMEN MCRAE MEETS
THELONIOUS MONK

Minton's, a Harlem nightclub, was home in the early 1940s for young musicians who were—it initially seemed—not so much expanding as dismantling jazz traditions. Charlie Parker, Dizzy Gillespie, Bud Powell, and Kenny Clarke, among others, were creating jagged, explosive, continually surprising rhythms and dizzyingly complex harmonies that seemed to collide with themselves. The melody? It was there, somewhere, if you could piece together the fragments as they whizzed by.

But there was a melodist among them. Pianist-composer Thelonious Monk was as disdainful of mass popular taste as his colleagues were; but as startlingly unexpected as his rhythms and harmonies were, his melodic lines were so clear, strong, and often witty that they stayed in the mind.

In the early 1950s, although most of the earlier pioneers were now playing downtown for slightly more money, Minton's was still alive. I started going up there to hear the intermission pianist, Carmen McRae, who played there occasionally.

She also sang, just as she played—crisp, precise (you could hear the commas in the lyrics), with a sure, playful beat. Then as now, she had the bearing of someone who had no patience with small talk, small minds, or people with intrusive personal questions. When pressed beyond annoyance, she could shoot you with her eyes.

McRae had been intrigued by Thelonious Monk's music from the time Minton's had been the modern jazz equivalent of King Arthur's Round Table. She had been married to the pervasively influential modern drummer Kenny Clarke, and so, she says, "I was in on the ground floor." For a long time, there were those— older jazz critics, for instance—who found Monk's pieces and playing strange, forbidding, lacking a center of gravity. McRae, however, found that reaction incomprehensible. "His music," she told me recently, "made me smile."

For a long time she had wanted to make an album of Monk's works, with lyrics added, but she doubted that any record label would be interested. RCA/Novus, however, proved her wrong, and the resulting album is *Carmen McRae: Carmen Sings Monk.*

Preparing to record the album, McRae listened to tapes of his recordings "for hours and hours—in my car, in hotel rooms on the road, in my bed at night. I lived with that music."

Getting inside the music meant that she had to learn "how the melodies were really meant to go, not the way I thought they went. In fact, nothing went where you thought it was going to go." Her knowledge of the piano—which included five years of classical studies starting when she was eight—helped a lot in understanding how Monk constructed his lines and chords.

"I'm sure," she says now that the album is done and she's including some of the songs in her concert repertory, "that Monk never had a vocalist in mind for his songs. If he had, he wouldn't have made them so hard."

On the album, she doesn't sound as if Monk is any harder to sing than Jerome Kern. In all these years, I've never heard Carmen McRae sound anything but coolly self-assured. Sometimes she's been too cool, as if the music wasn't worth her full attention, but here she's clearly enjoying the experience of being challenged by Monk's music.

With a wit as crisp and pungent as Monk's, she illuminates the fun in some of the songs. A far more accomplished musician than many singers, she is able to become a member of the band, not just a singer, without trying to imitate an instrument. Her natural phrasing and time blend with those of the sidemen. And her presence is so authoritative that it might have impressed the inscrutable Monk himself.

The songs include such essential parts of the Monk canon as "Well, You Needn't," "Rhythm-a-ning," "Ask Me Now," "Pannonica," "Ugly Beauty," "'Round Midnight," and "Straight, No Chaser."

The lyrics—by Jon Hendricks, Sally Swisher, Abbey Lincoln, Bernie Hanighen, and Mike Ferro—are not candidates for anthologies. But like her good friend Billie Holiday, McRae has a sound, phrasing, and time so arresting that the lyrics take on connotations the writers never had in mind. Also, there is the powerful undertow of Monk's music.

"Everything fits so well in Monk's work," John Coltrane said, "once you get to see the inside." The inner voicings and rhythms. These are compositions, not just tunes.

When his music was going good, Monk would get up from the piano and dance. Some said it was to make his rhythmic imperatives clearer to his musicians. Some said that he was just feeling so good he had to move. There are many passages in this set during which it's difficult not to move.

PART IV
the nonpareils

THE LIMITLESS MINGUS

In his life, as in his music, Charles Mingus was continually surprising himself, let alone his musicians and listeners. His very physical size changed from time to time as his weight ballooned and then shrank. So too, smiling, he could be as gentle as a shy suitor and then suddenly cause the entire room to darken ominously, with his double bass muttering like a thunderbolt on the way.

This virtuoso bassist and leader was one of the relatively few jazzmen to leave a distinctive body of original compositions—as have Jelly Roll Morton, Duke Ellington, and Thelonious Monk. Moreover, like Ellington, whom he greatly admired, Mingus composed specifically for the particular players who were with him at any given point. He then insisted that when they improvised on his themes, they simultaneously respect the essence of his music while also bringing their own ideas—fresh ideas—into their solos.

As one former Mingus sideman put it, "He just wouldn't let you coast." In a nightclub or in a concert hall, moreover, Mingus, on occasion, would put the audience on hold, stop the music, and berate his sidemen either for having gotten lost or for playing it safe in their solos by indulging in all-too-familiar licks. And there were times when he would lecture the audience too if it was not paying attention—or the right kind of attention. One night at a

New York club, he was trying out a new piece, full of demonic cries and shouts and roaring climaxes. At the back of the room there was some bibulous laughter in the wrong places.

Mingus stopped the music. "If you think this is weird," he said, "just take a look at yourselves."

He had some hard times, some of his own volatile making and others because he was very public in denouncing exploitative practices in the business end of jazz while also questioning the qualifications of most jazz critics—by name.

Yet for all his contentiousness, Mingus went through life with the ceaselessly high expectations of a romantic. There was a perennial boyishness, almost innocence, that was the underside of his querulousness when things went wrong. They weren't supposed to go wrong. Even Jim Crow, as furious as it made him, did not turn him into a separatist. Mingus could actually see, somewhere ahead, generations that, like jazz musicians, listened to individual voices and not group colors.

Most jazz musicians reacted swiftly to any form of racism, whomever it came from. (Exceptions, in those years, were trips through the South, when survival was the priority.) I saw Charles Mingus knock a white man out with one punch. The man hadn't said anything explicitly racist, but the attitude was very much there, and Charles, expecting the racist to strike sooner or later, decided there was no point in continuing the discussion.

Yet Mingus—who spoke out more plainly and fiercely about the exploitation of black musicians than anyone else—also went beyond race.

"It's not only a question of color anymore," he told me. "It's getting deeper than that. I mean it's getting more and more difficult for a man or woman to just love. People are getting so fragmented, and part of that is that fewer and fewer people are making a real effort anymore to find exactly who they are and to build on that. Most people are forced to do things they don't want to most of the time, and so they get to the point where they feel they no longer have any choice about anything important, including who they are. We create our own slavery."

Of his many albums, Mingus preferred *Tijuana Moods*, recorded in 1957 but not released until five years later. RCA has made this volcanic set available again. Better than that, in addition to the original LP, there is a second album containing alternate takes. And since Mingus was always reshaping his imagination, the alternates are as challenging as the takes originally released.

All the music in the album, as Mingus put it, "was written during a very blue period in my life. I was minus a wife and in flight to forget her with an unexpected dream in Tijuana."

New Tijuana Moods (RCA/Bluebird) consists of Mingus's recollections, bereft of tranquility, of his journey into the night world of his antic soul. While achingly tender in places ("Flamingo"), much of the music pulses with exhilarating, sometimes ecstatic rediscovery of all the senses that can be played in sensuous counterpoint. Mingus was a most resilient man.

Climaxing the climaxes is "Ysabel's Table Dance," which, said Mingus, "sums up all we could buy in Tijuana. It includes the far-out striptease—spots in the music played by the piano represent the scantily clad woman spinning from table to table, reaching her hand out for tips . . . or what-have-you." Mingus's music—always abounding in energy—is ferociously high-spirited in "Table Dance" and for much of the rest of the set. He was, as he said, "starved" for intimations that there could be more to life than a lost wife.

All the players were up to Mingus's demands that they enter into his memories while contributing their own. Dannie Richmond, who had just learned to play drums and was to be the fiery rhythmic core of all Mingus's subsequent groups, had been Mingus's companion during that tour of the night, and he sounds it.

Jimmy Knepper, the most resourceful trombonist in jazz, was a shrewdly observant ex post facto participant, as was the penetratingly passionate Curtis Porter (Shafi Hadi) on alto saxophone. A mysterious figure on the date, trumpeter Clarence Shaw, disappeared from the jazz scene soon after, much to Mingus's sorrow, for he was affectingly spare and subtly inventive. As Mingus said of Shaw, "He breathed good and deep for his ideas."

Mingus was afflicted, years later, with amyotrophic lateral sclerosis (Lou Gehrig's disease). The last time I saw him, he could no longer walk or play his bass, but he could still talk—and think of the pieces he wanted to write that were crowding his imagination. He died, looking for life, in Cuernavaca, Mexico, in 1979.

MEMORIES OF THELONIOUS MONK

In 1990, *The Chronicle of Higher Education* reported that the Thelonious Monk Institute of Jazz would open the next year in Durham, North Carolina, and be affiliated with Duke University. (Monk, an utterly uncategorizable pianist-composer, was born in Rocky Mount, some ninety miles from Durham.)

Seeing the news reminded me of an afternoon in the 1950s in Thelonious Monk's apartment in the San Juan Hill section of New York's West Side, near what is now Lincoln Center. The most imposing presence in the small quarters (after Monk) was a Steinway baby grand. Nellie, Monk's wife, noted that the instrument "takes up most of the living-room part of the kitchen."

That day Monk, for a while, was more talkative than usual. At other times his silences could last an hour or two or longer. A brilliant young musician, Gigi Gryce, came rushing in during one of the silences and said to Monk with great delight, "I got in! I got in! I'm going to Juilliard!"

After about ten minutes, Monk looked at the still radiant Gigi and said, "Well, I hope you don't lose it there."

"It" was the most important thing in jazz: the sound of yourself. A way of moving and shaping music so that if anybody turned on the radio in the middle of a performance, he'd know it was you. Could that be taught in a class?

When Monk's music was played, there was never any doubt as to its source. Pee Wee Marquette, the small, round, vinegary man who used to act as the town crier at Birdland, would introduce Thelonious as "the onliest Monk."

He played the piano with affectionate respect for the vigorous two-handed Harlem stride pianists of previous generations; but although he too covered the whole piano, Monk played—as he composed—with a spare, angular, often sardonic unpredictability of line, harmony, and rhythm. His beat could be like a tidal wave, and at times it pushed him up from the piano seat into a whooping-crane dance in front of his combo. Even when he stayed seated, Monk's legs under the keyboard engaged in what looked like a ferocious kazatsky competition.

Except for Duke Ellington, no one else in jazz has left as extraordinary and continually intriguing a body of compositions. Eleven of them can be heard—played by the composer with various combos—on *Thelonious Monk the Composer*, part of the generally impressive Jazz Masterpieces series on Columbia.

Some of the most internationally renowned works in the Monk canon are here: "'Round Midnight," "Brilliant Corners," "Well, You Needn't," "Blue Monk," "Crepuscule with Nellie." Although there is plenty of room for improvisation by Monk and his colleagues, each piece is precisely structured. Monk not only knew what he wanted from his musicians, he refused to accept anything less. Gigi Gryce once told me: "I had a part Monk wrote for me that was impossible. I had to play melody while simultaneously playing harmony with him. In addition, the intervals were very wide. I told him I couldn't do it. 'You have an instrument, don't you?' he said. 'Either play it or throw it away.' And he walked away. Finally I was able to play it."

If, during an improvised solo, a sideman forgot whose music he was playing as he flew into the wild blue yonder, he might never be able to return. One night, at the Five Spot in New York, I watched John Coltrane get off the stand after a set with Monk. Coltrane looked dazed and dismayed. "I lost my place," he said, "and it was like falling down an open elevator shaft."

For a long time, Monk—who had been at the creation of modern jazz with Charlie Parker, Dizzy Gillespie, and other frontiers-men and women—was treated by many jazz critics as a semi-comic eccentric rather than as an original. And that diminished his chances to work. I went with Monk to a class at Columbia University given by one of those critics, and the session began with the lecturer asking Monk, "Would you play some of your weird chords for the class?"

Monk was hurt and angry. "What do you mean weird? They're perfectly logical chords."

Eventually, he made many recordings and played a growing number of festivals and clubs. But Monk began to stay more and more within his own mind. The silences grew much longer, and for some years before he died in 1982 at the age of sixty-four, Monk did not play at all.

One night, before he had entirely given up communicating with the world, I spent an evening at the home of his friend, Baroness Nica de Koenigswarter, a world-class jazz aficionado who died in 1990 at the age of seventy-four. The baroness and I were playing some records by Ornette Coleman, who was getting a lot of attention and praise at the time. Monk, staring straight ahead, had said nothing for a long time. Suddenly, he interrupted a record. "That's nothing new. I did it years ago." Monk got up and started to go through the piles of Nica's records, without envelopes, stacked on the floor. He found what he wanted, played his old performance, which made his point, and said, "I think he has a gang of potential though. But he's not all they say he is right now. After all, what has he contributed?" And then Monk said nothing more for the rest of the evening.

Monk knew his own stature. At a recording session, when Coleman Hawkins asked Monk to explain some of his music to him and to John Coltrane, who was also on the date, Monk looked at the magisterial Hawkins: "You're the great Coleman Hawkins, right? You're the guy who invented the tenor saxophone, right?" Monk turned to Coltrane: "You're the great John Coltrane, right? Well, the music is on the horn. Between the two of you, you should be able to find it."

THE ONLIEST BIRD

I was not an immediate convert to the careening jazz of Charlie Parker. Starting in the mid-1940s, most of the younger musicians looked to Bird as the messiah who had come to deliver jazz from the cul-de-sac of the swing era. There were too few surprises in the music anymore, they said.

The awe in which they held Bird was distilled by the usually reserved John Lewis (who later became musical director of the Modern Jazz Quartet). He told of a 1946 Jazz at the Philharmonic concert with Lester Young, Willie Smith, and other formidable veteran jazz improvisers. Charlie Parker was also on the stand, and said Lewis, "Bird made a blues out of 'Lady Be Good.' That solo made old men out of everyone on stage that night."

In 1946 I had a jazz radio program in Boston, and Duke Ellington, Ben Webster, Johnny Hodges, and scores more classic jazz musicians didn't seem a bit old to me. Parker, on the other hand, played too many notes too fast. He was, moreover, too complex, and his tone lacked the fullness and warmth of Johnny Hodges. It was as if Bird was in too much of a hurry to care about tone.

One evening, in the radio studio, a musician took a 78-rpm

Bird recording and placed it on a transcription table that moved at 33⅓ rpm. "Now, listen," the musician said. "It's slow enough for you to hear what Bird is doing, to hear how he shapes his ideas. And listen to what he finds in the chords. Jazz is never going to be the same after him."

I did hear more than I'd heard before, and as I began to listen to Bird in clubs, I finally understood why musicians were transcribing his solos and following him around in the fierce hope that they could find out how to sound like him, be like him.

Being like Bird, as some of them discovered, was like burning the candle whole. He had a huge appetite for drugs, and he was so unreliable that international jazz impresario Norman Granz hired someone to track him during a Jazz at the Philharmonic tour to make sure he'd make the evening concert. A musician who managed Bird for a time said that being with him over a long period was "like having a terrible disease."

Much of the time Bird was in a panic, strung out, with no money. And yet there were nights, many of them, when he played with a stunning, seemingly endless flow of fresh, soaringly cohesive ideas and enormous passion. His time, his jazz time, was intricately connected to all the other nuances of his phrasing and harmonic textures, and yet he swung with explosive spontaneity.

There were other nights when it was embarrassing to hear him fumble and to watch his eyes, which were somewhere else. "I don't let anyone get close to me," he once said. When he was down very low, he'd look at random for help. Not long before he died in 1955, I was coming down the stairs at Birdland around two in the morning and Bird was coming up. I'd interviewed him a few times through the years, but we had never hung out together. Tears were streaming down his face, and he told me, "I've got to talk to you, it's very important. Very important."

"Okay," I said, "we'll go into the coffee shop on the corner," and I started to turn around.

"No," he said, "I'll call you tomorrow." He didn't, and I hadn't thought he would.

Bird was a myth in his own time. Icarus with a magic horn and a mocking monkey on his back. Posthumously, he has become even more of a mythical presence, as players all over the world, on all instruments, search for ways to get inside his way.

For years there has been another myth, the holy grail of the lost Dean Benedetti recordings of Bird's improvisations in various clubs. Benedetti was a young saxophonist obsessed with Charlie Parker, and with Bird's permission, he recorded him at clubs in Los Angeles and New York in 1947 and 1948.

I had heard of these alleged additions to the Bird canon for years and finally decided that if they had ever existed, they'd disappeared forever or somebody had recorded over them. But these recordings are not merely the stuff of legend. They have now been released by Mosaic, the nonpareil jazz-archivist label, in boxed sets of ten LPs (35 Melrose Place, Stamford, CT 06902).

There are two caveats. Benedetti did not record on anything like what was state-of-the-art equipment, even in 1947 and 1948. So some of the sound is as bad as it was in some of the clubs Bird played. On the other hand, there are enough passages that do not generate more frustration than pleasure. In sum, for those who are fascinated by Charlie Parker—and they are legion among jazz romantics and musicians—the set will bear many playings.

Another caveat is that since Benedetti was only interested in studying what Parker was up to, he generally stopped the machine as soon as Bird was done—and sometimes that means only a fragment of a song, although most of the takes are longer. The experience is disconcerting. It's like hearing a performance of *Henry V* that has only the voice of Laurence Olivier. To paraphrase William Saroyan, there is no context all down the line.

But there is Bird—on nights when, as they used to say, he was really cooking. And on other nights when, as they also used to say, he could have sent his suit. But those nights when he was all together, at least on the stand, were exhilarating. One joyous climax after another. It was what happened off the stand that turned Bird into such a desperate old man so soon that he never found out what more he could do on his horn and with his life.

Once he was telling me with great enthusiasm about listening again to Bartók's Second Piano Concerto: "I heard things in it I never heard before. You never know what's going to happen when you listen to music. All kinds of things can suddenly open up. But when I hear my own records, I hear all kinds of things I should have done. There's always so much more to be done in music. It's so vast."

One of the astonishing things about Bird is that he actually did so much before he finished the job of destroying himself.

The Sunday afternoon before he died, Bird was to have played at the Open Door—a large, cheerless room in a drab, past-caring-to-care section of Greenwich Village. He had played there several times before at Sunday sessions. This Sunday he played not at all. He made an appearance, but all the time he was there he ignored his horn. At one point a friend, another musician, found him in the men's room. Bird was looking at himself in the washroom mirror. He was slowly, carefully, and firmly putting himself down in a conversation with the face in the mirror. He went on for some time, adding the newcomer in an old trialogue. Finally Bird looked hard at the mirror and harshly called the image the worst enemy he had. But, the other musician observed drily, "you'll never have a friend closer to you than that." Bird laughed and went out into the club. But he didn't play.

When Bird died, among the listed causes of death were stomach ulcers, pneumonia, advanced cirrhosis of the liver, and a possible heart attack—the attending physician, basing his judgment on the physical condition of the corpse, estimated Bird's age as between fifty and sixty. He was thirty-four.

DIZZY IN THE SUNLIGHT, I

Cheraw, in northeastern South Carolina, figured briefly in the history of the Civil War. There was a Confederate supply depot there, which was captured by General William Tecumseh Sherman during his scorched-earth march through the South.

Cheraw is much better known now as the birthplace of John Birks Gillespie. There's a Dizzy Gillespie Drive there. He used to go back from time to time, and one afternoon a couple of years ago, I asked him if the place had changed much when it came to Jim Crow.

"There are nice people down there," Dizzy said, "but you have to be careful because you're still colored." And he told me about going down for a day not long before.

"I was on my way to the mayor's house—I knew all the mayors over the years, most of them from when they were kids. He was giving a cocktail party for his sister who lived in San Francisco. I asked if I could bring a couple of my cousins, and he said to bring whomever I wanted.

"So everything was cool. I needed a haircut. There were two black barbershops. We stopped the car before each of them, but they were all filled up with people waiting, so I told my cousin to take me to the white barbershop. He say, *'What!'* I say, 'Take me to the white barbershop, and let's see what they say.'

"We walked in the door. Only the barber was in there. No customers. He didn't look up. I said, 'I'd like a haircut, please.' Then he looked up for a second and said, 'I'm sorry, we don't cut colored hair.'

"I figure I'm going to show my class by just turning around and walking out. Here I am in the South Carolina Hall of Fame, and the year I won that, there were two others who got in—General William Westmoreland and Father Joseph Bernardin, who became a cardinal. So, me being in that Hall of Fame with the military and religion, I thought I was ready for something. At least a haircut.

"As I turned to go, the barber takes another look and says, 'I know you.' I just walked out, and when I told the mayor, he said, *'What!'*"

Dizzy smiled. "It got in the papers."

We were talking about Charlie Parker. I asked Dizzy what he found so different about Bird's music when he first heard him. "His phrasing," Dizzy said. "And his bluesiness. He played blues better than anybody. I mean, he played blues like T-Bone Walker would sing, and then Bird would put some little extra things in there. He was the most fantastic musician I ever heard."

I may have missed it, but I don't recall any of the obituaries having mentioned that Dizzy himself was a hell of a blues player. He was very conscious and proud of his roots in the music. That's why one day when I casually talked about the revolution in the music created by him, Bird, Thelonious Monk, and others, Dizzy corrected me: *"Evolution,"* he said, "not revolution."

Another time, I mentioned that the day after Charlie Parker died, Art Blakey said that the second tragedy was that young people in America—black as well as white—didn't know who Charlie Parker was.

"Yeah," Dizzy said. "As a kid, I didn't get taught my heritage. I went to a segregated school, the Robert Smalls School. In that public school, I never heard of Robert Smalls. I wondered where this name had come from. But later, I found this guy was black, one of the great Americans."

In the new paperback edition of *There Is a River: The Black Struggle for Freedom in America* (Harcourt Brace Jovanovich), Vincent Harding tells of an event in South Carolina during the Civil War: "One audacious group of [black] families under the leadership of a skilled black harbor pilot, Robert Smalls, actually commandeered and sailed the *Planter*, a Confederate coastal supply ship, past the unwitting Southern keepers of the Charleston harbor batteries, and delivered it—and themselves—into Union hands."

On one of his trips to Africa—in Benin, West Africa—Dizzy was made a chief. "They made me both an artist and a chief. Double respect, man. My great-grandmother was the daughter of a chief.

"When I went to Nigeria, I saw my family there. I saw in the faces there my brother, my mother, my father."

Art Taylor, one of the continually inventive jazz drummers, compiled an illuminating book of conversations with musicians, *Notes and Tones* (Perigree Books, published by Putnam). In his conversation with Dizzy Gillespie, Taylor asked him about his religion. Said Dizzy: "I belong to the Baha'i faith. Baha'i means follower of Baha'u'llah'. Baha'u'llah means 'glory of God' in Persian. The one principle that holds true in the Baha'i faith is the unity of mankind. Everything you do is designed to bring about the unity of mankind. So that's what I'm about now."

In one of our conversations, I also asked about the Baha'i faith, many of whose adherents have been murdered during the 150 years of the religion's existence—especially in Iran, where the religion began. The rulers of that nation, who maintain that their religion is the holiest of all, are still executing Baha'is.

The faith, Dizzy told me, "teaches that God has had a special plan for mankind on earth for all these billions of years, and that plan has been moving, moving, moving. Each period in our spiritual development, he sends a manifestation of himself. He picks somebody out from the people here on earth, and he tells him what to say to the people about the way to live with your fellow man. The message changes as we get more knowledge.

"So he sent these guys—Abraham, Moses, Jesus, Muhammad, Buddha, Krishna, Zoroaster. And each of them would start a religion, an evolving religion. Eventually, mankind will become unified, when there is a world government and everybody belongs to it and you don't need a passport. There'll be an international language taught in all the schools, and all your important papers will be in that language.

"This should take another one thousand or two thousand years. But on the way we get little pinches of unification. The League of Nations was another little pinch. So was the United Nations."

"And jazz?" I asked.

"Yeah, yeah. That really is a pinch of unification. It makes me feel really good to belong to jazz, to that part of society."

I knew Dizzy for some forty years, and he did evolve into a spiritual person. That's a phrase I almost never use because many of the people who call themselves spiritual would kill for their faith. But Dizzy reached an inner strength and discipline that total pacifists call "soul force."

He always had a vivid presence. Like they used to say of Fats Waller, whenever Dizzy came into a room, he filled it. He made people feel good, and he was the sound of surprise, even when his horn was in its case.

But in later years there was also a peaceableness in Dizzy. There was nothing passive about it. It was his soul force that resolved tensions.

For example, in the 1980s, there was to be a concert at Lincoln Center honoring Dizzy. He and a big band were, of course, to be at the center of the celebration. A few days before, I went to a rehearsal. Everyone was there but Dizzy.

No music was being played. The only sounds were a bitter argument between Max Roach and Gerry Mulligan. Each had some compositions on the program, and at the start the argument was about who was to have more of his pieces played. Then it became very personal and poisonous.

The other musicians, all of them renowned, either looked down at their music in embarrassment or found a place on the ceiling in order to avoid, God forbid, meeting the eyes of the combatants. The tension in the room got fiercer and fiercer.

In the back, Dizzy, who had not moved, was watching. Then he strode to the front of the band, spread out a score, and said, "Letter B, we'll start at letter B."

He had filled the room with reasonableness without getting involved in the battle. Most of the leaders I've known through the years would have scolded the antagonists for wasting valuable rehearsal time and acting like children. But Dizzy, by his very presence, had broken the tension.

Of course he had, for so many years, earned the respect of the musicians, but so had other leaders, who would have added to the tension. Softly, being able to relax now, an alto saxophonist blew the rest of the bad feelings out the door, as he played "I'll Always Be in Love with You." Even Max and Gerry laughed.

Dizzy used to say that of all the awards he'd received, he was most proud of the Paul Robeson Award from the Institute of Jazz Studies at Rutgers.

"I was a great fan of Paul Robeson," he told me.

"What made him one of your heroes?"

"He wouldn't capitulate. He wouldn't back down. And he wouldn't be corrupted by money or by anything else."

Paul Robeson was a classic victim of McCarthyism except that—as Dizzy emphasized—he refused to play the victim. Robeson was denounced as a Communist by the right-wing press, which was in abundance. He lost work and for years couldn't accept engagements overseas because the State Department denied him a passport.

"He was so great at so many things," Dizzy said. "A great sports figure, a lawyer, an actor, a singer. So many things. I don't see how he had the time to develop all those qualities.

"He heard us play at the Apollo. He wrote me a note and said he'd enjoyed it so much. And then he said that he would have liked to come backstage and tell me personally how much he'd liked the performance. But he didn't want to cause any trouble."

"You mean he was afraid that being there would cause you trouble with the FBI as someone who knew him?"

"Yeah, something like that. I called him up, and I said, 'Paul, for you to come backstage and tell me you liked the performance, I'd be willing to go to jail.'"

DIZZY IN THE SUNLIGHT, II

When I first heard Charlie Parker, I said, "That's how our music should be played . . . " I'd never heard anything like him. It was scary! After we got it together, yeah, I knew we were making something new. It was magic. Nobody on the planet was playing like that but us.

—Dizzy Gillespie, *San Francisco Chronicle*, May 25, 1991

All of the music is out there in the first place, all of it. From the beginning of time the music was there. All you have to do is try to get a little piece of it. I don't care how great you are, you only get a little piece of it.

—Dizzy Gillespie, in a conversation with this writer, 1983

Dizzy was talking about Bird. He had always given Charlie Parker great credit, the major part of the credit, for the invention of modern jazz. But Dizzy made far-ranging original harmonic and rhythmic contributions—and continued to long after Bird died. Dizzy, however, saw Bird as the primary source.

Duke Ellington told Dizzy, by the way, that the biggest mistake Dizzy had made was to let people, namely critics, call that music bebop. "From the time they name something," said Duke, "it's dated."

As Duke predicted, some of bebop has become dated. But not the music of the originators. A few months ago I put on a Charlie Parker record for the first time in quite a while. I was stunned once again by the torrent of ideas—fresh, original, brilliant ideas—and the depth of his time. Bird is no more dated than Duke or Lester Young. But Duke was right about the name.

"Charlie Parker was brilliant," Dizzy said one afternoon. "And not only in his music. He was a very serious guy. He knew a lot about politics and other things besides music."

"You could tell that sometimes," I said, "but at other times, he was a wholly different person. There were many Charlie Parkers."

Dizzy nodded. I told him about an interview I'd had with Bird on a radio station in Boston. His answers were only grunts as he flipped through *The New Yorker*. A few months later, also on the radio, Bird wouldn't stop talking. He told me about a session he was planning with woodwinds, a choral group, a harp, and a rhythm section. "Something," he said, "on the line of Hindesmith's *Kleine Kammermusik*. Not a copy or anything like that. I don't want ever to copy." He also gave an incisive analysis of Bartók's Second Piano Concerto.

"He was just a phenomenon," Dizzy said, shaking his head. "Nobody knew where he got what he had." And nobody knew how to keep him from destroying himself. During one of his last nights anywhere, Bird ran into Dizzy. "Save me! Save me!" he said. By then, Dizzy didn't know how.

"Would things have been different for Charlie Parker," I asked Dizzy, "if he'd had a Lorraine?"

At his death, Dizzy had been married to Lorraine for fifty-two years. And for fifty-two years he had carried their marriage certificate in his pocket. Dizzy dedicated his remarkably candid, multivoiced, essential book, *To Be Or Not to Bop* (Da Capo paperback) to Lorraine: "Her love, help, humor, and wisdom. Her unselfish and unswerving devotion made me the man and musician I wanted to be."

It was clear from the start of Dizzy's courtship with the former dancer that "if I wanted to marry her, I would have to walk the straight line." Dizzy kept walking that line while some other musicians lost control of themselves and lost everything else.

Another thing about being married to Lorraine, Dizzy told me, was that "she does not want to be wrong. So I just let her be right all the time. That's a harmony that works—you just be wrong all the time." Dizzy laughed.

"But could it have made a difference with Bird—if he'd had a Lorraine?"

"I guess that would have depended on him. If he'd have been willing to do what I did for her—walk the straight line."

There are many stories about Dizzy, but the one that most graphically captures a particular dimension of Dizzy's way of throwing bigots off balance is in *Jazz Anecdotes* (Oxford University Press) by Bill Crow, a first-rate bassist who is also an invaluable chronicler of the jazz life.

"In 1958," Crow writes, "George Wein arranged to stage a jazz festival at French Lick in southern Indiana. He demanded and received assurances that there would be no discourtesies shown the black musicians and fans who would be visiting this former lily-white resort. . . . When the Gerry Mulligan Quartet arrived there, however, Art Farmer and Dave Bailey expressed doubts about using the swimming pool. They wanted to avoid any ugly scenes.

> From the lobby the blue water of the pool looked inviting, and Art and Dave had just about decided to get into their swimsuits when Dizzy Gillespie stepped out of the elevator. He was wearing bathing trunks from the French Riviera, an embroidered skullcap from Greece, and embroidered slippers with curled-up toes that he'd picked up in Turkey.
>
> A Sheraton bath towel draped over his shoulders like a cape was fastened at the neck with a jade scarab pin from Egypt. With a Chinese ivory cigarette holder in his left hand and a powerful German multiband portable radio in his right, he beamed cheerfully through a pair of Italian sunglasses.
>
> "I've come to integrate the pool!" he announced. He led the way to the poolside beach chairs, enthroning himself in one with plenipotentiary panache. After he had the

attention of everyone at the poolside, he grabbed Jimmy McPartland, who had also come down for a swim. Arm in arm, the two trumpet players marched to the diving board and jumped in together, and the last barrier to integration at French Lick was down.

Dizzy integrated all kinds of scenes. On a State Department tour, the band was in Karachi, Pakistan, and Dizzy was fascinated to see a snake charmer in the park. "I had my horn there, and I saw him playing and the snake moving, moving. So he say to me, 'Come on, come on.' I went and got next to him, and he say, 'Go on, go on, play something.' I started playing "Groovin' High," and the snake was going and going, and the snake charmer say, 'Move your horn a bit.' I must have put that horn too close. The next thing I hear was, 'sssshhhhlllllick!' And the snake was *moving*. I broke the record for the backwards jump. I must have jumped back nineteen feet."

Dizzy still wanted to learn more about that powerfully moving music. He invited the snake charmer and his companion up to his hotel room.

The hotel manager was aghast. Not at the snake, but at the fact—he vigorously pointed out—that the snake charmer was of a decidedly lower caste than the establishment's clientele. Dizzy, who could be the stubbornest man on the planet, insisted. "The man's a musician, isn't he?" he told the manager. And so, in that hotel room, duets were played before an audience of one suspicious, ever-vigilant snake.

Dizzy liked to tell another story about one of his missions for the State Department. ("I used to do a lot of apologizing for what the State Department had done.") This happened in Ankara, Turkey, where a lawn party had been arranged at the American embassy. The climax was to be a jam session presided over by Dizzy. "While I was signing autographs," he recalled, "I happened to look at this fence surrounding the grounds. A lot of street kids were pressed against the fence. They wanted to come in and hear the music. One of them actually climbed over the fence, and a guard threw him right back over it.

"I asked what was going on. Why did they do that? And some official said, 'This party is for select people. Local dignitaries and important Americans in the city.'

"I said, 'Select people! We're not over here for no select peo-ple! We're over here to show these people that Americans are all kinds of people.' I had a girl in that band, and almost as many whites as blacks. We had a good mix.

"The ambassador comes over and asks, 'Are you going to play?' I say, 'No! I saw that guard throw a little kid over the fence. Those are the people we're trying to get close to—the people *out-side* the fence.'

"So the ambassador said, 'Let them in, let them all in.'"

And that is how John Birks Gillespie brought democracy to the American embassy in Ankara.

In all the years I knew Dizzy, I rarely heard him put anybody down. But there were exceptions. In Arthur Taylor's book *Notes and Tones*, Dizzy said, "History will either off you or make you valid. History has wiped Stan Kenton out completely. They thought he was a master, they thought he was greater than Duke Ellington, and that motherfucker couldn't even keep time."

Most of the time Dizzy had a lot of fun and was fun. But as he would tell you, he was very serious about his music. He was con-tinually looking for and finding new ways of shaping and color-ing sounds, and he was continually teaching what he found to musicians—of all ages. At the funeral service for Dizzy at Saint Peter's Lutheran Church, Hank Jones—a truly master pianist who himself is always searching—told of how Dizzy, through the years, would show him "chord inversions I hadn't even thought of."

Seeing Dizzy, however casually, was like coming into sunlight. By the warmth of his greeting, his natural considerateness, and the keenness of his intelligence—which made his wit so sharp—he was a delight to be with. And he was a delight to himself when he was all alone.

In *Waiting for Dizzy* (Oxford University Press), Gene Lees tells of arranging to meet Dizzy in a small park in Minneapolis so that his photographer could take some pictures. As Lees and the pho-tographer approached, they saw Dizzy, who did not see them.

"Lost in some musical thought, Dizzy was softly dancing, all alone there in the sunlight."

"EVERY NIGHT, I BEGIN AGAIN"

In the Ellington sense, pianist Hank Jones is serenely beyond category. If I owned a nightclub, I'd give Jones a lifetime contract. Unlike some musicians who memorize attractive "licks," as they used to be called, Jones is a true improviser. His is "the sound of surprise," to use Whitney Balliett's phrase for jazz as it ought to be.

Furthermore, Jones is a melodist, a lyrical storyteller. "In a way," he told me recently, "I have a singing approach to the piano. I play very long lines that connect with each other to tell a musical story. The sentences become paragraphs, and as for the colors—well, the harmonies are what the lines are built on."

In my nightclub—although there would also be bass and drums and visiting singing horns—I would ask Jones to play a solo set each night. A complete pianist, he needs no rhythm section to keep him swinging. Indeed, I know of no jazz musician on any instrument with such instantly natural and flowing a jazz pulse, no matter the tune, the complexity of the chords, or the tempo.

A particularly pleasurable recording of this protean pianist is *Hank Jones: Live at Maybeck Recital Hall* (Concord Jazz).

Maybeck Recital Hall in Berkeley, California, is actually, said

Jones, "a large house with a cathedral ceiling in the main room. And that room is small but with remarkable acoustical properties. The cathedral sound has such presence."

The program includes a good many standards, because Jones, preferring a piano that sings, is especially fond of the storytelling composers of the 1930s and '40s. From that period and others, he brings precise immediacy to "The Very Thought of You," "What Is This Thing Called Love?," "Memories of You," Thelonious Monk's "Blue Monk" and "'Round Midnight," and "A Child Is Born," by his brother, the late Thad Jones.

Hank Jones is the oldest of three brothers—all of whom helped shape jazz history. Originally from Saginaw, Michigan, the Joneses became a notable part of the Detroit jazz scene. Thad, a buoyant trumpet player, later became coleader of a resourceful big band with the late drummer Mel Lewis. Elvin Jones, a fiery, often mesmeric drummer, has influenced many of the younger percussionists. He played with the passionately demanding John Coltrane for a long time and has since headed his own groups.

Thad was a commanding presence, both as a leader and trumpet player. Elvin Jones also projects seemingly boundless energy. Their pianist brother, however, is soft-spoken, rather shy, unfailingly courteous and seemingly without even the mildest eccentricities. He is, as the gravel-voiced Symphony Sid used to say on his New York radio programs, "a gentleman of jazz."

But at the piano Hank Jones is a joyful swinger, and so compelling a chronicler of the privacies of love that the music sounds autobiographical. What he does not reveal about himself in conversation comes through in his music. That could be said, of course, about many musicians, from Count Basie to Ellington.

Nonsolo CDs by Hank Jones on Concord Jazz include *Rockin' in Rhythm*, with bassist Ray Brown and drummer Jimmie Smith, and *Lazy Afternoon*, with drummer Keith Copeland, bassist Dave Holland, and Ken Peplowski on alto saxophone and clarinet.

Jones plays with musicians of all ages and styles because he always has. As a youngster, he broke in with bands in Michigan and Ohio and went on to play with Andy Kirk, Coleman Hawkins, and Norman Granz's tumultuous Jazz at the Philharmonic. He spent five years with Ella Fitzgerald, toured often with

Benny Goodman, and in recent months has traveled through Europe with Dizzy Gillespie and in Japan with his own trio.

I've listened to Jones in clubs and on records, and it often sounds as if he is playing a song for the first time, although I've heard him do the same tune often.

"Well," he said, "there's always something new to explore in music. There are infinite ways of playing a song, and I keep trying ways I hadn't thought of before."

I mentioned what Dizzy Gillespie had once told me: "Music is so vast, so endless, that nobody can get more than a small piece of it. You just keep trying to find more than you've already found."

Jones nodded. "That's exactly right," he said. "That's why every night, I begin again."

THE SOLITARY FLOATING JAZZMAN

The man died on May 30, 1977. According to the *New York Times*, he left no immediate survivors. A neat man who went off like the Cheshire cat. ("I've often seen a cat without a grin," thought Alice, "but a grin without a cat!")

After Paul Desmond's death, some friends met at a Columbia Records studio where the Dave Brubeck Quartet had made many of its recordings. Paul's music played softly in the background. There were a few short speeches and stories about him, all low-key, some very funny. The piano had been tuned, but nobody had played. Then, from the back of the room, a wiry, graying man, wearing a golf hat and a quizzical look not unlike Paul's, moved almost at a run to the piano and said, "This is a song Paul always asked for."

Jimmy Rowles played "Darn That Dream," fitting it to Paul's tone and floating beat. He got up, did a small jig, and uttered a cry. Not in mourning. It was what Thomas Wolfe called a goat cry—to life. To Paul's music.

So much for no immediate survivors.

•   •   •

I first saw the cat and the grin in 1952. He was playing alto with the Brubeck Quartet. Brubeck, utterly without guile or humor, a man of invincible innocence, played the piano as if he were clearing a lifelong trail through a forest of giant sequoias. Paul Desmond leaned against the piano, hands folded over his cunning axe, and seemed to be in reverie amid the hearty clangor. An amiable solitary at the revival meeting.

Then, long-legged, lean, bemused, he approached the microphone and transformed the night. With an insinuatingly pure tone, he spun cool, sensuous, melodic variations on the theme of the moment; although Brubeck was still fighting Indians in the background, Paul drew the audience into another, more gentle fantasy. Romantic but not sentimental. We were too hip for sentimentality in public. His was the realm of an urbane dreamer all too aware of how close yearning is to feeling ridiculous.

Certainly there have been more original and more searing alto saxophonists in jazz, but Paul had this particular turf to himself. He could put you in a trance, catch you in memory and desire, make you forget the garlic and sapphires in the mud. And there was more. At times Paul was the wittiest of improvisers. His ear was extraordinarily quick and true, his mind moved with eerie swiftness. He could take a phrase that someone had played earlier or a musical reference that a friend in the audience would understand and insert it into his solo. He'd build on that phrase until he had turned it inside out and seven other ways. Usually this kind of quoting is trickery, but Paul made it cohere. In his music, as in his life, the absurd cohabited with the familiar.

For several years Paul was the closest friend I had. We always found more to talk about than there was time. Books, writing (he very much wanted to be a writer), music, movies (he had "discovered" Ingmar Bergman and other European filmmakers before the rest of us). And women. We were both in love with Audrey Hepburn. (He did something about it, writing and recording "Audrey," but there was never a response from that finespun lady.) I was so fond of Paul that I even forgave him for introducing me to my former wife.

When Paul left Brubeck in 1967, I thought he would have the

time to start a career as a writer of humor. And he intended to. His letters from the road—glumly hilarious accounts of rustic plagues visited upon itinerant jazz musicians—showed he had the requisite skill. But Paul took writing so seriously that he would not try to publish anything unless he believed it was perfect. So, little was written, less sent out—a few liner notes and one classic road story. The story, which appeared in the January 10, 1973, issue of *Punch*, tells of a New Jersey state fair at which the Brubeck quartet played alongside a horse show. ("For Chrissakes, could you tell the drummer not to play so loud? He's terrifying the horses.")

Paul did go back to music and made albums that belie the *Times* obituary. The best is *The Paul Desmond Quartet Live* (A&M/Horizon), and there is also a surprisingly luminous collection of duets with Dave Brubeck on A&M/Horizon. No sounds of trees falling: Brubeck, too, seemed to have fallen under Paul's gentling, reflective spell. It is, quite simply, an album to make love by. A use Paul would have appreciated, though he would never have suggested it, not wishing to intrude.

Paul and I had not seen each other for a long time. No particular reason. We relayed messages through musicians but somehow didn't directly connect. I followed his music and hoped he would get to the writing. Then, one night, after Big Joe Turner's opening night at the Cookery, Charles Mingus and I went to hear Jimmy Rowles at Bradley's. Paul was there, the grin the same, though he looked tired. We enthusiastically exchanged phone numbers and intentions. But since both of us were clearly immortal and I always had too many deadlines, I never made the call.

It was cancer. Three packs a day. In the last months, Bradley Cunningham (the owner of Bradley's) used to spend some time at Paul's apartment. Bradley is craggy in appearance and gentle of soul. "Paul used to leave the door open," Bradley told me. "He was so weak that he figured if he needed help, people should be able to get in without any trouble."

One morning Charles Mingus decided to visit Paul and cheer him up. Mingus didn't know that it had been many, many years since Paul had awakened before three in the afternoon. It was a day on which Mingus felt like cutting a bold swath through the world, and so he came uptown in a black Spanish cowboy hat and a heavy, swirling black cape.

In through the door strode this imposingly grave figure. Paul, his eyes opening, struggled to focus on the apparition and then, sorting through memory, found the hooded harvester in Ingmar Bergman's *The Seventh Seal*. "Okay," Paul said to Bradley Cunningham, who was standing near his bed, "set up the chessboard." And grinned.

THE FALL OF A JAZZ TRUMPETER

The calls came late at night, when the club he was playing was dark, or when he was depressed and not playing at all. Woody Shaw, a trumpet player and composer, was sometimes seized with a consuming desire to talk in questions. They were seldom about music but rather about politics, racism, and existence (like Duke Ellington's song "What Am I Here For?").

The conversations were challenging, like his music. I never could be sure what would be around the next corner he took. At the time, in the late 1970s, Woody Shaw had earned great respect among musicians who had heard him with, among others, Joe Henderson, Art Blakey, and combos of his own. Miles Davis, never known for easy praise, said of Shaw: "Now there's a great trumpet player. He can play different from all of them."

Woody played both in and out of the mainstream modern jazz tradition—hard bop and also freer music that made structural sense, unlike the chaotic flummery of some of the "experimental" players of the time. His temperament was essentially lyrical, as was that of a key influence, Clifford Brown. Woody could be exultant and reflective and always played with total authority. He often improvised lines that danced, and his tone was warm and crisp.

Dexter Gordon, with whom Shaw worked, said, "The thing about Woody is he's done his homework. He's hip to Louis Armstrong and covers the whole spectrum." Shaw named his son Woody Louis Armstrong Shaw.

Born in North Carolina in 1944, he grew up in Newark, New Jersey. His father had sung with the Diamond Jubilee Singers, thereby deepening his son's roots through gospel music. But Shaw was also curious about the European tradition and became a skilled classical trumpet player. He wanted to go to Juilliard, but, he told Chuck Berg in an interview: "I couldn't have gone because I didn't graduate from high school." He had dropped out to go on the road with a jazz band.

Shaw influenced a number of young players who heard him in clubs and on records. Wynton Marsalis, shortly after he joined Art Blakey's Jazz Messengers in 1980, applied for—and was awarded—a grant to study with Shaw. Recently, alto saxophonist Antonio Hart paid tribute to Shaw in his Novus/RCA album, *for Cannonball and Woody*—particularly in appreciation of Shaw's use of wider intervals than had been customary among trumpet players. Those leaps have since been further developed by Wynton Marsalis.

For all the esteem in which he was held by musicians, Woody Shaw never broke through in terms of big record sales. The 1970s was an ormolu age of fusion and funk in jazz, and Shaw would have none of either.

Along with the diminishing momentum of his career, by the early 1980s he had gone through the breakup of his marriage. He died in 1989. Jazz-record producer and historian Michael Cuscuna—a longtime friend of Shaw—recalls: "While recuperating from depression and resulting substance abuse at his parents' home in Newark, he ventured into Manhattan to see Max Roach at the Village Vanguard. By the early morning hours, he was alone in a Brooklyn subway station when he fell into a passing train, which resulted in a lost arm and, after months in the hospital, his death in May 1989.

"Whether his eyesight (he was legally blind from retinitis pigmentosa, which he had all his life) or New York Transit's random violence caused the accident is something we will never know. And no, it was not suicide, as anyone who knew Woody can tell you."

Cuscuna is one of the principals of Mosaic Records, which produces expert reissues of otherwise unobtainable records. A lasting achievement by Mosaic is *The Complete CBS Studio Recordings of Woody Shaw* (three CDs; Mosaic Records, 35 Melrose Place, Stamford, CT 06092).

Woody Shaw used to recall that when his future seemed limitless, Freddie Hubbard and Lee Morgan, both much-esteemed jazz trumpet players, told him he would be the next great jazz horn in the line of Louis Armstrong, Roy Eldridge, Dizzy Gillespie, Miles Davis, and Clifford Brown.

Listening to Woody on trumpet, fluegelhorn, and cornet throughout these 1977–79 performances on the Mosaic set affirms the judgment of Hubbard, Morgan, and Miles Davis—even if most of the jazz public didn't catch on.

Much of the music consists of originals by Shaw, but there are also standards. Among the young sidemen are musicians who have since become figures of jazz consequence, such as trombonist Steve Turre and drummer Victor Lewis. Woody Shaw's is the dominant voice. With acute musical intelligence, daring, lyricism, and a constant compass, he brings it all together.

I miss those late-night calls. They were not complaints. They were questions. And Woody Shaw left us with the hardest question of all. What was he doing in that Brooklyn subway station? And how did he fall?

THE IMPRESARIO WHO BROUGHT
CIVIL RIGHTS TO JAZZ

In 1994 Verve Records presented a Carnegie Hall concert celebrating the fiftieth anniversary of Norman Granz's career in music. Granz created the Jazz at the Philharmonic tours as well as a series of record companies that never abandoned jazz, no matter what the trends were. And starting long ago, he absolutely refused to play to segregated audiences.

Black musicians used to have a store of war stories about the risks to body and spirit when they were booked in the South and, for that matter, other parts of the country, including New England. Managers, booking agents, and promoters had no interest in changing local mores, so long as the money came in.

In many places on tour, black musicians, after working segregated clubs and dances, were barred from white hotels. And often, to get something to eat, they had to commission a white man to buy sandwiches for the band.

Richard Boyer, in a 1944 *New Yorker* profile of Duke Ellington, told of a policeman in Jim Crow St. Louis greeting Ellington enthusiastically and saying, "If you'd been a white man, Duke, you'd have been a great musician." With his customary regal manner, Duke, smiling, answered coolly, "I guess things would have been different if I'd been a white man."

Norman Granz, the most stubborn and brusque man I have ever known, went into jazz to attack racial discrimination head on. He loved the music, but as he said in Dizzy Gillespie's book, *To Be Or Not to Bop*, "The whole reason for Jazz at the Philharmonic was to take it to places where I could break down segregation and discrimination. . . . I insisted that my musicians were to be treated with the same respect as Leonard Bernstein or Heifetz because they were just as good, both as men and musicians."

"With Norman," trumpet player Clark Terry once told me, "everything was first-class. The travel, the hotels, everything. He had deep pockets. The other promoters had short pockets."

And everything out front had to be exactly the way Granz wanted it to be. He once described his strategy for bringing Jazz at the Philharmonic to racist Houston in the 1950s. After renting the auditorium, "I'd hire the ticket seller and tell him there was to be no segregation whatsoever. Well, that was new for Houston. I removed the signs that said WHITE TOILETS and NEGRO TOILETS. That was new. The ticket seller was a Texan and I knew he didn't have eyes to do what I'd asked him to do, but he was getting paid, so he had to."

When Granz and the players came—among them Dizzy Gillespie, Ella Fitzgerald, Buddy Rich, and Lester Young—there were white ticket purchasers who suddenly realized they might have to sit alongside black Texans. Granz told them, "You sit where I sit you. You don't want to sit next to a black, here's your money back." Granz's shows included a lot of jousting among the players—what used to be called "cutting contests." Because of the anticipated excitement, JATP attracted large audiences. When you have a strong show, Granz would say, you can lay down some conditions, including in Houston.

An intellectual, Granz can be a very provocative conversationalist on topics from jazz and race relations to the whited sepulchers in political office. Another of his passions is art. He was a friend of Picasso and has an impressive art collection in Geneva, Switzerland, where he now lives in semiretirement at seventy-five. Characteristically, he did not attend the Carnegie Hall concert in his honor. He never liked ceremony. At his own concerts, he would stride onstage, quickly give the names of the players, though not his own, and rush off.

Years ago, when Granz was in the USSR, an *Izvestia* reporter asked him which musician most typifies jazz. Without hesitating, he named the trumpet player Roy Eldridge. "He's a musician for whom it's far more important to dare, to try to achieve a particular peak—even if he falls on his ass in the attempt—than it is to play safe. That's what jazz is all about."

These years Granz may be somewhat of an anachronism, as a dedicated integrationist and as a man who doesn't hesitate to dare to keep his principles alive. The present NAACP, with its overtures to Louis Farrakhan and the Nation of Islam, probably would not take any note of him now. Nor would he of it. Granz never had any patience with retreats into separatism. He was not a sentimentalist. He just knew what would work and what wouldn't if the nation wasn't to slide back—because separate was never equal.

PART V
the classical players

RED ALLEN: "WHAMP! WHAMP!"

The first wave of modern jazzmen, with the exception of the antic Dizzy Gillespie, insistently demonstrated that theirs was serious music. They did not crack jokes on the stand. They seldom smiled. As John Lewis, who was later the musical director of the Modern Jazz Quartet, solemnly put it at the time: "For the younger musicians this was the way to react against the attitude that Negroes were supposed to entertain people. The new attitude of these young Negroes was: 'Either you listen to me on the basis of what I actually do or forget it.'"

Not even Louis Armstrong (but for whom some of these players would have been in another line of work) was exempt from these stern strictures. He had a "plantation image," said Gillespie back then. (Gillespie, some years later, said he had misjudged Satchmo. That Armstrong grin, Dizzy said, represented the musician's "absolute refusal to let anything, even anger about racism, steal the joy from his life.")

What many of the younger generation of players also ignored was that the jazz elders had grown up as entertainers and were not at all ashamed of pleasing audiences by reaching out to them. They had come up on the riverboats and in dives where it was often necessary to do something extramusical to capture the rowdy audience's attention, and they had often played at dances where the couples were very serious, but not necessarily about the music.

One of these "entertainers" was Henry "Red" Allen, who, in the years after the modernists came to dominate the jazz scene, received little recognition among modern jazz audiences for his musical inventiveness. I heard him almost every night for months at Boston's Savoy Café in the early 1950s and then later at the Metropole in New York, where he stood over a long, busy bar, prefacing each number with the thumping shout, "Whamp! Whamp!"

Around that time, a vintage trumpet player, Louis Metcalf, heard a young bopper say, as he listened to Red Allen, "Man, why doesn't that cat give up?" Metcalf was hurt: "Seems as though they want us to die out."

But there were new players who heard something in Red Allen that made them listen again. Gillespie recalls, "A few of the older guys started playing our riffs, like Henry 'Red' Allen. The others remained hostile to it."

But Allen had for a long time been creating new dimensions in rhythms and textures that influenced a number of the younger players. Miles Davis paid attention to him. And the avant-garde trumpeter/leader Don Ellis called Allen "the most creative player in New York."

There were nights when he came close to fulfilling that tribute. Allen could swing hard and deep, but sometimes with asymmetrical rhythms and only an implicit pulse, so that the time moved in unexpected ways. And he was a melodist, improvising new variations, and variations upon variations, illuminated by continually changing colors. Until it was time for "Whamp! Whamp!" again.

His credits were much more traditional than his playing. Trained in a New Orleans brass band led by his father, he worked with Fate Marable's Mississippi riverboat band, played with King Oliver and then with a big band led by Louis Armstrong. Allen went on to become part of the big-league orchestras of Luis Russell, Fletcher Henderson, and the Mills Blue Rhythm Band before leading combos of his own until he died of cancer in 1967. He was fifty-nine.

For all of his flamboyance as a combo leader (he worked the crowd like a master of ceremonies at a steamfitters' convention), Red was extremely shy off the stand. And very proper. I can't recall his ever swearing, in or out of the presence of ladies, and he was very sensitive to what people were saying beneath the words they used. He was a proud man. Gentle as he was, he suffered no slights.

One of the few critics to have recognized the scope and depth of the music that followed "Whamp! Whamp!" is Martin Williams. He wrote the notes for a serious—and, yes, entertaining—reissue set, *Henry 'Red' Allen: World on a String/Legendary 1957 Sessions* (Bluebird CD).

Among Red's colleagues were the magisterial Coleman Hawkins on tenor saxophone; J. C. Higginbotham, who played trombone the way Adam Clayton Powell talked; clarinetist Buster Bailey, like Higginbotham a longtime Allen associate; and a robust rhythm section particularly energized by drummer Cozy Cole and pianist Marty Napoleon—a true jazz enthusiast who hardly ever stopped smiling even when someone hit a clinker.

Martin Williams begins by saying flatly that "no one continued to explore and develop his talents and remain open to new ideas more than trumpeter Henry 'Red' Allen. The performances distill Allen's heritage, from New Orleans on." The songs range from "Love Is Just Around the Corner," "Ride Red Ride," and "Let Me Miss You, Baby" to "Love Me or Leave Me," "I've Got the World on a String," and "Sweet Lorraine."

Along with Red's twilight lyricism, there are his cracklingly dramatic up-tempo parades and his affectingly informal singing. On ballads, Allen was intimate without being sentimental. And on the blues, he sounded like he'd known all kinds but had never let them get him down for long. "Whamp! Whamp!"

A GENTLEMAN OF JAZZ

When jazz was young, it was considered a young man's game. Nightly improvisations without a net and the strenuous after-hours pleasures available to itinerant swingers were thought to be too much for old-timers. Indeed, according to the prevailing myth—given currency by Dorothy Baker's novel *Young Man With a Horn*—the most original players were spent before they even became middle-aged. Among those burning the candle all along its length had been Bix Beiderbecke, Bunny Berigan, and later, Fats Navarro and the Great Speckled Bird, Charlie Parker.

Over the decades, however, a lot of jazzmen kept on keeping on until they were older than the club owners and entrepreneurs who booked them. It has become commonplace to hear still-uncommon music by improvisers in their sixties, seventies, and even eighties. One of the most exhilarating, crisply swinging sets I've heard in years was by a band in a Greenwich Village club led by trumpeter Doc Cheatham, who was born in 1905.

In 1987, in the Great Hall of New York's Cooper Union, seventy-nine-year-old Benny Carter conducted the American Jazz Orchestra in a program of his compositions and arrangements, including a new, long work, and was the featured soloist on alto saxophone and trumpet. In all of his specialities that evening (he left his clarinet home), Mr. Carter was as effortlessly distinctive as he has been throughout a career that began sixty-five years before when the kid from San Juan Hill (where Lincoln Center now stands) went up to Harlem to sit in and learn from such masters as Willie "The Lion" Smith, the stride pianist and spinner of airy melodies.

Mr. Carter was not an apprentice for long. Playing with and arranging for Fletcher Henderson and McKinney's Cotton Pickers and then for his own orchestras, Mr. Carter developed a style of improvising and writing that was unfailingly lucid, lyrical, and elegant. The music also moved—Mr. Carter being an expert in setting and deepening an infectious rhythmic groove. Accordingly, everything he writes, no matter where it's played, is right for dancing.

Mr. Carter is regarded by musicians of all generations as the preeminent gentleman of jazz. He is courtly, solicitous of the views of his musicians (though after he hears them, he'll do what he wanted to anyway), and like Duke Ellington, he has apparently taken an oath never to criticize a living musician. Or a dead one. And he never appears in the least ruffled by unexpected circumstances of any kind.

One night years ago, at a Jazz at the Philharmonic concert, Mr. Carter was onstage with Johnny Hodges, Charlie Parker, then coming up, and other legendary horns. Mr. Parker, who was providing a new grammar for the playing of jazz, was explosively brilliant. Mr. Carter, who understood that new grammar, simply played Carter—a soaring, singing theme and ingenious streamers of variations that made it clear he was not going to be pushed into obsolescence by Mr. Parker or anybody else who came blazing along.

The evening at Cooper Union was of particular importance to Benny Carter because he had not had a chance to work with a big band for a very long time. He disbanded the last full-time orchestra of his own in 1946, vanquished by economics. At the New York concert, Mr. Carter was able to hear his music exactly as it had stayed in his memory.

The American Jazz Orchestra was created to bring back alive the compositions and arrangements of those who have created the written heritage of jazz. With such attentive and resourceful players as trombonists Jimmy Knepper and Britt Woodman, trumpeter

Marvin Stamm, pianists Dick Katz and John Lewis, tenor saxophonist Lou Tabakin, drummer Mel Lewis, and bassist Ron Carter, the evening was the first time in decades that the full scope of Benny Carter's writing, playing, and conducting had been heard. (A studio recording was made of the program by the Music Heritage Society.)

For a long time after he disbanded his orchestra, Mr. Carter, based on the West Coast, spent much of his energy writing for films and TV shows. With that kind of work "thinning out," as he puts it, he's been on the jazz road increasingly during the past decade. His stamina and the manifest pleasure he gets from playing further disprove the notion that there are age limits to the full-scale practice of jazz.

A couple of summers ago, at an open-air jazz concert in New York's Washington Square, Mr. Carter was trading choruses with Dizzy Gillespie and Dizzy's young protégé, Jon Faddis, a very strong trumpeter. The tourney of the horns went on for a long time, and Dizzy, finally out of wind, sank onto a chair. But Messrs. Carter and Faddis battled each other until the end. Benny looked as if he could have gone on for another hour.

Benny Carter has always listened to young players. Now that he conducts workshops at a number of colleges, he hears even more of them. "The kids are fantastically endowed with technique," he said recently on National Public Radio. "They do more today than I would have thought possible fifty and sixty years ago. But they sacrifice a lot of emotional content for technique. And skilled as they are, I can't tell one from another. There's something to be said for street knowledge, for going around and sitting in at clubs, as I did when I was young, when they let me."

Now many of the young players with remarkable, soulless technique are going into high schools to teach still younger players. It's similar to what Dylan Thomas observed when he first came to America. He wondered how the poets here could possibly learn enough about life to be poets—because after graduating from college they went right into another institution to teach.

The untenured Benny Carter, meanwhile, keeps enlivening the night throughout the world. After the Cooper Union concert he embarked on his eighth tour of Japan. He's accepting gigs as far ahead as anyone wants to book him.

A LEGEND WHO WON'T
ADMIT HE IS ONE

Many years ago I was interviewing a renowned, uninhibited jazz trombonist on the radio. He often ended a gig by mixing together all the drinks left on the tables into a huge nightcap that would have destroyed most lay drinkers on the spot.

The trombonist had brought his girlfriend to the studio, and while one of his recordings was playing, he ordered her to keep her eyes on the big clock on the wall. "Watch that second hand," he said. "Every time it moves, you've lost a second of your life." She was still staring when the program was over. So was I.

This was a time when many jazz players were not expected to live very long as the seconds ticked by. Bix Beiderbecke had died at twenty-eight, Bunny Berigan at thirty-four. And there were others who never came close to getting Social Security.

As time went by, however, there were more and more exceptions to the romantic notion that jazz players, like Icarus, were fated to fall early from the sky. Louis Armstrong and Duke Ellington, for instance, died in their seventies, and Benny Carter, as noted, is well into his eighties.

At eighty-nine, trumpeter-singer Doc Cheatham may be the

only musician still alive to have recorded with Ma Rainey and such other matriarchs of the blues as Clara Smith and Trixie Smith. He also, at eighteen, accompanied Bessie Smith. But his playing can't be categorized by any period. As he says, he has continued learning from jazz trumpet players all his life—from Louis Armstrong, Red Allen, Tommy Ladnier, and Bix Beiderbecke to such modern jazz improvisers as Clifford Brown and Fats Navarro, as well as newer figures of consequence such as Roy Hargrove.

As is consistently clear in Cheatham's Columbia CD, *The Eighty-Seven Years of Doc Cheatham* (He turned eighty-eight as the set was released), Doc is a lyrical performer, with a sure and supple command of dynamics, a flowing beat, and a sense of self-surprise that all durable jazz players have. "I find myself playing different every year," Cheatham says. "I can't understand it, but the new ideas still come to me."

What also makes Cheatham distinctive is that as a soloist, he is a late bloomer—a very late bloomer. For many years he was a lead trumpeter in such big bands as those of Cab Calloway, Teddy Wilson, Benny Carter, and Chick Webb. During that time Cheatham felt incapable of ever becoming a soloist in the same league with the horn men he so much admired. Also, as he pointed out during an interview on National Public Radio, "Being a lead trumpet player for so many years, I wasn't allowed to play solos, and it bothered me quite a lot. Nobody thought that I could play a solo. I was holding myself back. Being a soloist was locked up in my mind. I couldn't get it out until it just came out."

It finally came out when Cheatham, then sixty, was hired by Benny Goodman, who at the time was leading a small combo rather than a big band. Cheatham, therefore, had to take solos on every number. He discovered that at last he could be part of "all the beautiful trumpet sounds" he'd been absorbing from his heroes over the years.

Cheatham often worked with some of the more corybantic Latin bands—Machito and Ricardo Rey, among them—thereby strengthening his chops, as jazzmen used to say, and his confidence. A bristling, swinging Latin band propelled by exultant dancers is no place for any player who's holding himself back.

Doc Cheatham's singing, which can also be heard on his CD,

is laid back, urbane, and gently memorable. It is as if he were singing to himself, looking back on a lifetime of tunes, some of which were new when he was. Among the vocals are "Miss Brown to You" (long associated with Billie Holiday, whom Cheatham used to accompany) and his signature, "I Guess I'll Get the Papers and Go Home."

Also present are a powerful, deeply felt "Blues in My Heart," a rambunctious "Muskrat Ramble," and a "'Round Midnight" that confirms that Cheatham is a significant contributor to—as well as an inheritor of—the legacy of jazz trumpet soloists.

"When I turned seventy," he recalls, "I think I was on my way to being a better player." Feeling more satisfaction with his work, he nonetheless refuses to accept for himself the overall title of the Columbia series in which his CD is included: "Legendary Pioneers of Jazz." Cheatham emphasizes that Louis Armstrong is indeed a legend, but "people call me a legend just because of my age."

Cheatham has not thought of retiring. "Money doesn't bother me," he told *Down Beat*. "I just go along. I think everyone should be rewarded for what they do, [but] playing is just a part of me and I have enough of what I need. I'm satisfied."

When Doc was eighty-five, Dizzy Gillespie paid tribute to the survivor: "He's playing as good as ever. Cheatham never drank much, never used grass. He's a perfect example of what to do for longevity."

As a jazzman who didn't become a soloist until he was sixty, Doc Cheatham needed those bonus years. On Sunday afternoons, a good many New Yorkers and visitors go to hear him at Sweet Basil's on Seventh Avenue South in Greenwich Village. They don't come because of Doc's age. They come because he makes them feel good.

STARS AND NONSTARS

In a review years ago of a jazz reissue, I mentioned the singing tone and exceptionally graceful lyricism of alto saxophonist Hilton Jefferson. After decades of traveling with big bands, the only steady job he could find at the time of the review was working as a bank guard. His wife wrote me, saying how pleased he had been to see his name. He thought just about everybody had forgotten him.

While the legendary figures of jazz—Coleman Hawkins, Lester Young, Roy Eldridge, and others—are remembered and revered, many of the supporting players feel abandoned in their autumnal years. There are no more recording dates, and if they get weekend gigs, they play in clubs that critics never visit. The widow of one musician—a clarinetist who played with the force of a trumpet and the imagination of a storyteller who never ran out of surprises—swears he died of neglect.

Although there are many pleasures in an enormous PolyGram Mosaic set, the twenty-one-LP *Complete Keynote Collection*, the most surprising are likely to be those provided by a pride of supporting players of the past. Their classic jazz improvisations are as enlivening as they were in the 1940s when these sessions were made.

Among them are Hilton Jefferson and trumpeter Joe Thomas,

whose warm, clear sound and effortless swing quickened the bands of Fletcher Henderson and Benny Carter, among others. Even when Mr. Thomas was working regularly, he was so often called "underrated" by jazz writers that after a while it seemed to be part of his name. Another trumpeter on some of these dates, Emmett Berry, was a quiet man with a big sound and delicate phrasing. He, too, is seldom mentioned anymore, except in the more recondite jazz journals.

The presence of these and other distinctive nonstars on many Keynote sessions reflects the commendable and always nontrendy tastes of the late Harry Lim, the producer of the dates. Born in Java, at the time part of the Dutch East Indies, Mr. Lim went to school in Holland, and early exposure to recordings by Red Nichols revealed his vocation to him: he had to find something to do with jazz. Hearing Louis Armstrong's "West End Blues" confirmed his calling.

When he came to the U.S. at the age of twenty, Mr. Lim almost immediately started producing jam sessions and then recordings. The Keynote sessions in this set were made between 1941 and 1946 and include much previously unissued material, from newly discovered dates in the archives to alternate takes.

While I suppose that historians will be grateful for the comprehensiveness of this huge undertaking, had I been the editor, the twenty-one LP's would have been reduced by five or six. But there is much to celebrate in the rest.

The musicians in this very big box are by no means limited to the undeservedly neglected. Members of the jazz pantheon are also present: Coleman Hawkins, Roy Eldridge, Jack Teagarden. And there is a high-spirited quartet session led by Lester Young with drummer Big Sid Catlett, who could intuit what everyone in the group was thinking. Young also takes a full half of an LP with a septet that includes trumpeter Buck Clayton, trombonist Dicky Wells, guitarist Freddie Green, and drummer Jo Jones. The four titles—"After Theatre Jump," "Six Cats and a Prince," "Lester Leaps Again," and "Destination K.C."—are the very model of the joy of jazz. And the alternate takes demonstrate how improvisations are shaped and reshaped in the self-editing process that differentiates long-winded jazz ramblers from the exact master players.

Producer Lim also found studio time for an alto saxophonist who has long been forgotten by all but a few fans of a certain age. Pete Brown, a round man who seemed to live mainly through his horn, which he played as if he were bobbing on a not-too-calm sea but enjoying the experience enormously. His delight in surprising himself is infectious. There are also subtle, almost whispering interplays of temperaments and textures in sessions led by xylophonist Red Norvo.

By contrast, on a Bud Freeman date, Edmond Hall, another vintage jazzman who is hardly ever recalled in print these years, reveals why many musicians considered him the hottest of all clarinetists. Yet while he played with a passion that sometimes nearly overwhelmed his trumpet and trombone colleagues in the front line, Hall could also move inside a ballad as if he were disclosing confidences that he wouldn't even tell his wife.

Hall, like all the musicians here, was proud of his high-risk profession. It was and is ceaselessly competitive, and while its practitioners hardly ever used the term, they knew it was an art. And since it was an art, they didn't expect large audiences and big money. But they did figure on a certain amount of recognition as long as they were around.

Many were disappointed, but *The Complete Keynote Collection* does bring back to life some of their daring music.

THE CLARITY OF BUCK CLAYTON

In 1934, trumpeter Buck Clayton—originally from Parsons, Kansas, not a renowned jazz center—was leading a big band in Shanghai. He was twenty-three years old. It was two years later, however, as a sideman with Count Basie, that Mr. Clayton began to develop an international reputation as a jazz original.

Even in a band with such nonpareil improvisers as Lester Young, Dicky Wells, and Herschel Evans, Mr. Clayton was equally distinctive. He effortlessly created clear, singing melody lines, and his sound was both full and crisp. He was one of those players who, if asked to demonstrate how not to swing, couldn't have done it. In his solos even the silences pulsated.

Buck Clayton had something extramusical going for him as well. An exceptionally handsome man, he could have become— had the Hollywood studios then been of a mind to integrate the silver screen—the first black matinee idol. As it was, traveling with Basie back then, he knew there were two nations long before the Kerner Commission did. Being in Charles Delaunay's jazz discography didn't change that.

Mr. Clayton stayed with Basie until 1943. Then he went on tour with Jazz at the Philharmonic and various groups overseas and headed his own combos. He had done some arranging and composing during all those years, but in 1978 he learned that if he were to stay in jazz, it would be solely as a creator of lines and harmonies for other people to play. A dental condition had made playing increasingly painful, with a bridge cutting deeper and deeper into his lip. An operation didn't help, and the sound of that singing horn could now be heard only on records.

In the years since, Mr. Clayton has written for various ensembles but always hankered for a group of his own that would play his music the way he heard it. In 1986 he assembled a thirteen-piece band—four saxophones, three trumpets, two trombones, and a rhythm section. It has performed at the Village Vanguard and the Cat Club in New York and at the Nice Festival in France.

Both live and on the band's first album, *A Swingin' Dream* (Stash Records), Buck Clayton distills the essence of swinging. Most of the musicians are in their early thirties, with impressive jazz resumes, and although they grew up in the bop era, they play Mr. Clayton's scores with manifest delight. One test of whether a band is cooking, as musicians used to say, is whether the players smile a lot during a set. Some of Mr. Clayton's musicians seem to find it hard to stop grinning.

Such originals by the leader as "Margaux," "Beaujolais," "Avenue C" (which he wrote for Basie), and the deep, slow, sensuous "Black Sheep Blues" invite the players to swing. The writing is spare, with emphasis on deceptively simple and hummable melodies. And with all the space that Mr. Clayton leaves, it's impossible for soloists to hide behind thickets of notes. When each player stands up alone, he has to have something personal and melodic to say.

By contrast, much of the newer jazz has been described admiringly by *New York Times* critic Peter Watrous in a review of a saxophonist who began a solo "that contrasted blunt, drawn-out melodies with inkblots of sound, flurries that ran off into split tones." Also in the set were saxophonists who "rant and rave ferociously" and a "duet, tense with clashing microtonal inflections."

Nearly seventy-eight, Buck Clayton is regarded with respect by some of the younger musicians but is considered to be of another time. Yet the music I heard at the Village Vanguard was not in the least anachronistic. Indeed, after listening to many "inkblots of sound" and other "microtonal inflections" in advanced jazz performances where the beat can't be felt, let alone heard, I find Buck Clayton's jazz as fresh as an April day after a cold and crabbed winter.

Also, and I suppose this *is* anachronistic, Buck Clayton's music can be danced to. One problem is finding clubs where there still is dancing, and then people who know how to dance to a swinging beat—rather than moving as if they'd been plugged into a light-bulb socket.

Mr. Clayton, in any case, is pleased at having his own band to write for. He sits at a table next to the bandstand, rising to announce each number, then—as in his scores—giving only as much direction as is needed. "I get such a kick," he told me one night, "out of having what I write played by musicians who feel the music the way I do."

Of other jazz, the advanced kind, Mr. Clayton says that he wonders at the absence, by and large, of melody, and the presence of so much writing. "They don't know what notes to leave out," he said, which reminded me of Dizzy Gillespie saying, "It's taken me most of my life to know which notes not to play."

One afternoon, Buck Clayton told me of a conversation he had had with Count Basie about a year before Basie died in 1984. "We were talking about trumpet players who used to be in the band. Me, Harry 'Sweets' Edison, and others. Then Basie said, 'Damn it, I'd give a thousand dollars to find a trumpet player who doesn't play so many notes.'"

"I'VE GOT TO FEED MY FACE"

It was during the Great Depression. I was eight, in bed with the radio beside me. Searching the dial, I found a broadcast from the Hotel Sherman's Panther Room in Chicago. The announcer—after describing the plush surroundings—introduced Fats Waller, who then said to me and who knows how many thousands more, "I wonder what the poor folks are doing tonight."

I liked his music that night, but I also never forgot those first words I heard him say. Soon his recordings were on the radio a lot in Boston, and for months a disk jockey played the same Fats Waller song every morning just before I went to school. It was "Your Feet's Too Big," and it always made me laugh, especially the end: "Your pedal extremities really are obnoxious! One never knows, do one?"

By the time I left grammar school, I was hooked on jazz and found out that this "harmful little armful," as Waller described himself, was a powerful presence in the music. A pupil of James P. Johnson, he was, when he chose, a stunning two-handed stride pianist who influenced Art Tatum and Count Basie, among others. And he was an astonishingly prolific composer: "Ain't Misbehavin'," "Honeysuckle Rose," "Squeeze Me," "Blue Turning

Grey Over You," "Keepin' Out of Mischief Now," and one of the simplest and yet most haunting melodies in all of jazz, "The Jitterbug Waltz." There were many more.

I was a freshman reporter for my college paper when I saw that Fats Waller was coming to town. I didn't think I'd have a chance for an interview. What could it mean to him to be noticed in the paper of a college he'd probably never heard of—Northeastern? He turned down my proposal of interviewing him in his hotel room and instead invited me to dinner.

As the courses followed one another, I imagined this was what it was like in the Panther Room. I had to keep on reassuring him that I'd had enough.

A few weeks before, I'd heard a solo organ album, recorded in Europe, on which Fats played spirituals and some classical pieces. I told him how much I liked it and was sort of surprised that the album was nonjazz all the way.

"That's my first love, you know," he said. "The organ." He told me that Marcel Dupré, the master organist, had enabled him to play the organ at the church of Saint Sulpice in Paris. Built in 1776, it was considered the finest organ in the world. Fats said he wanted to record more classical organ works. He'd been much taken with classical music since he was fourteen, when his father took him to Carnegie Hall to hear Ignacy Padereweski. And his teacher, James P. Johnson—a master of the stride piano and a composer—had also studied and greatly enjoyed classical music.

Since I was only sixteen, I asked Waller why, if he loved the organ so, he didn't just take more of his time to play what he wanted to on that instrument.

Waller looked at me in a way that showed I needed instruction. "You see," he said, "I've got to feed my face."

Not that he suffered any internal torment in being an entertainer. It would have been impossible to fake the joy he took in mocking the white-bread lyrics of the novelty tunes he had to record from time to time. And he was naturally gregarious. Louis Armstrong said, "I've seen Fats Waller enter a place, and there was a gladness in the faces of all the people in the joint. And Fats wouldn't be in the place a minute before he would tell them a fine joke and have everybody holding his side from laughter."

Still, occasionally Waller would keep alive his hope of playing other kinds of music too. Guitarist/singer Marty Grosz, whose performances have more than a little of Fats Waller's spirit, writes that "before a 1940 record date organized by guitarist Eddie Condon, Fats warmed up with Debussy, but when the red light went on he galvanized the band with some of his barrelhouse piano."

There is now a cornucopia of Fats Waller CD reissues on RCA's Bluebird label. Fats Waller doesn't date. The immediacy of his warmth and irresistibly swinging beat are as satisfying as they were then. Also still fresh are his interpretations of lyrical, introspective pieces. He could range from the rambunctiousness of "The Joint Is Jumpin'" to the graceful "Clothespin Ballet."

The best single CD is *The Joint Is Jumpin'*, which includes both Johnson's "Carolina Shout" and "Your Feet's Too Big." A two-CD collection, *Fats Waller Piano Solos/Turn on the Heat*, reveals why he was so great a force among jazz pianists. Among the tracks are his perennially attractive "African Ripples" and "Clothespin Ballet."

The Middle Years (1936–38) is a three-disk set including "My First Impression of You" and "Blue Turning Grey Over You." Another three-CD collection—Waller was in the studios a lot—is *The Last Years (1940–1943)*. Among the pleasures are "Fats Waller's Original E-Flat Blues," "'Tain't Nobody's Biz-Ness If I Do," "Pantin' in the Panther Room," and "The Jitterbug Waltz."

He had a boundless appetite for food and drink but little patience for sleep. Yet he did die in his sleep—from pneumonia and from enthusiasm. It happened on the Santa Fe Chief, hurtling through Kansas, in 1943. He was thirty-nine.

Years ago, Fats Waller's son, Maurice, told me that his father had left a considerable number of compositions that had never been published. "Some are finished," he said. "Some are not. Half of them don't have a name. They weren't commercial; they weren't the type of thing he was supposed to have done. It was a matter of his getting at his inner self in them."

THE EDDIE CONDON
REPERTORY COMPANY

An astonishing event for jazz buffs happened in 1944. NBC's Blue Network started a weekly radio series of undiluted hot jazz under the tart, laconic direction of entrepreneur/rhythm guitarist Eddie Condon. Such an event would be just as astonishing today, whether on American radio or television. For regular network broadcasts of jazz, you have to go to Germany, England, France, or Japan.

Fortunately, nearly all these historic Blue Network sessions were put on transcriptions. (Most were later rebroadcast by the Armed Forces Network.) Listening to two of the volumes, now reissued on the Jazzology label, reminded me why, as a boy, I found such pleasure in jazz, and have ever since.

Eddie Condon shunned written arrangements. You agreed on a key, you set the tempo (at which he was an expert), and then it was all a sunburst of surprises. All you needed were one-of-a-kind improvisers who knew how to fit in with other singular swashbucklers.

So, week after week on the Blue Network, there was such jazz royalty as Harlem stride pianists James P. Johnson and Willie

"The Lion" Smith. The Lion, who was black, also spoke Yiddish on the side (though not, alas, on these broadcasts). Among the musicians was Edmond Hall, the most fiercely swinging clarinetist in jazz history. By contrast, Benny Goodman sounded like a civil servant.

Also on that long horn was Pee Wee Russell, who was so original that the shapes of his solos were utterly unpredictable. It often sounded as if each chorus were being played in a minefield. Or, as some of the regulars at the bars he played used to say, "How the hell is he going to get out of that one?" And there was Pee Wee's tone. To steal Lee Wiley's description of Billie Holiday, Pee Wee sounded like his shoes were too tight. But as with Billie, the man's acute musicianship, whimsical yet mordant imagination, deeply swinging time, and that unforgettable tone all came together in solos that, to this day, are lyrical beyond category and fashion.

The songs include traditional anthems that used to be played at Sunday jam sessions throughout the land and at night in such clubs as Nick's in Greenwich Village: "That's A-Plenty," "Wolverine Blues," "I'm Coming Virginia," "I Found a New Baby," and "Royal Garden Blues." I heard those and others in the tradition many times when this kind of unfettered jazz had something of an audience, and I never tired of them because each time even the ensembles never sounded quite the same.

It seems almost impossible for this genre of jazz ever to come back, although a couple of years ago I did see a classroom of college jazz musicians surprise themselves by tapping their feet and laughing in pleasure when their instructor slipped a Dixieland recording into his lecture. (It was a jazz style entirely new to them.) But they quickly regained their properly serious attitude toward America's original art form.

What comes through splendidly in the Blue Network Condon sessions is the sheer, uninhibited pleasure the musicians experienced in those wide-open settings: strutting trumpeters Max Kaminsky, Oran "Hot Lips" Page, and the perennially underrated Jonah Jones; the crisp, silvery Bobby Hackett on cornet; trombonists Benny Morton and Bill Harris; and the energetic drummer George Wettling, who, as I recall, also was a student of that sunny painter, Stuart Davis.

It wasn't all bobsled jazz. Lee Wiley, the cool sensualist, appears on Volume 2 in "I've Got a Crush on You" and "Sweet and Lowdown." There is an affectionate tribute to Bix Beiderbecke ("In a Mist," "Davenport Blues," and "Candlelight") that distills the incorrigible romanticism of that too-fun-loving American original.

The music on these records was best characterized by Bix, who said to an apprentice jazz player one night: "One of the things I like about jazz, kid, is I don't know what's going to happen next. Do you?"

"A FRESH, HAPPY LOOSENESS"

In March 1988, for the first time in its distinguished but little-known history, the Commodore Music Shop—and Commodore Records—became famous. While hosting the Grammy Awards on CBS, Billy Crystal affectionately recalled his part, as a boy, in the Commodore story.

Mr. Crystal is the only big-league comic with a deep, family attachment to jazz. As a kid, he got to know many of the sempiternal swingers, and in one of his standard monologues—which he performed on the Grammy telecast—he turns into one of the black musician-mentors of his youth: "Can you dig it? I knew that you could."

Billy Crystal's father, Jack, managed the Commodore Music Shop, located at Forty-second Street and Lexington Avenue in Manhattan. It was a nondescript shrine for jazz buffs from everywhere. During my first week in New York in 1953, I made a pilgrimage there to buy collectors' items; to listen to the hip customers, some of whom were musicians on the very records I had just bought, and to ask information of Jack Crystal. He was a dour-looking man, spare with words, sharp of eye, and possessed of a dark humor for those who paid close attention.

The elder Crystal ran boisterous weekend jazz sessions at the

Central Plaza on Second Avenue with the now legendary Sidney Bechet, Henry "Red" Allen, and Wild Bill Davison. Beer flowed from big pitchers as a cooling obbligato to the hot sounds. It was during those nights that young Billy Crystal became impressed for life with "those guys—their attitude; their hipness; the way they dressed; the way they never wore anything real tight."

Jack Crystal's boss at the record store was Milt Gabler. Like Jack Crystal's son, Mr. Gabler was much taken with those guys who invented music as they went along. "They've got such big souls," Mr. Gabler once said. In 1938, he formed Commodore Record Company. Why not sell in his shop recordings made to his taste? And in other shops as well?

Milt Gabler was not a musician, but years of listening had taught him the difference between hot and hokum. Also, because he genuinely admired the musicians he selected, Mr. Gabler created an easeful ambiance in the studio. Jazzman Richard Sudhalter described "a fresh, happy looseness" at the Commodore sessions.

As a boy in Boston, working after school to finance my obsession with jazz, I had bought each red-label Commodore as it came out. They were $1.50 each, a lot of money for a recording then, but they sure were special. Unlike pop sides, whose life spans were like those of mosquitoes, the jazz on Commodore was forever.

In recent years, as new listeners to jazz have become curious about its fabled past and older aficionados have wanted to go home again, the Commodore sessions have reappeared from time to time with new alternative takes, previously issued sides, and the unalloyed original releases. One recent celebration of the music's undiminished zest is *52nd Street Swing: The Commodore Years* (available in various jazz specialty stores).

The music begins with a session that made me shout with the shock of unfiltered pleasure when I was thirteen (much to the consternation of my mother): Chu Berry and Roy Eldridge swinging so hard that they drew me, or so it felt, right into the grooves. There follow the explosive Coleman Hawkins, the vastly underrated trumpeter/vocalist Hot Lips Page ("Gee Baby, Ain't I Good to You"), and Billie Holiday.

Lady Day sings one of her few blues, "I Love My Man." ("I ain't good-looking and my hair ain't curled/But my mother gave me something/That's going to carry me through this world.")

There is an entire session of The Kansas City Six, an effortlessly lyrical, floating ensemble of Count Basie sidemen and friends. Of particular enduring interest is the clarinet playing of tenor saxophonist Lester Young. He used a metal clarinet, as I recall, but his tone is warmer, mellower, and more singing than that of any other clarinetist in jazz history.

Among the jazzmen who used to appear at the Second Avenue jam sessions as well as on the Commodore label was clarinetist Edmond Hall, heard here in characteristically pungent, intensely absorbed and absorbing form. The gentlest of men off the stand, Hall played with a sense of wild wonder at how transcendent music-making can be.

There are other tributes to Milt Gabler's taste (Don Byas, Big Sid Catlett, Jonah Jones, Ben Webster). But also present are a rackety couple of tracks with Gene Krupa and Charlie Ventura, along with tepid dates led by Red Norvo and Eddie Heywood. Still, there are so many triumphs of the guys with big soul that the set is worth having and protecting.

The Commodore Music Shop is gone, as are Jack Crystal's weekend jam sessions on Second Avenue, but the spirit of the music makers is as brawny and tender as ever in these recordings. They created great pleasure, now as then, and unbeknownst to them, they also helped create Billy Crystal.

"I CAN NEVER SAY
ALL I WANT TO SAY"

Roy, or "Little Jazz," as the trumpeter is often called, was the most competitive player in the music. He loved jam sessions—a form of after-hour jousting in which young players dreamed of making their reputations by outdrawing such top guns as Roy. Eldridge was seldom bested. One of the few who finally outlasted him one night was Dizzy Gillespie.

Dizzy recalls that Roy was always at the ready for musical combat. "He'd take out his horn at the door and start on a high B-flat, coming up on the bandstand, walking with it."

Eldridge was incapable of coasting. I once helped put together a jazz hour for CBS-TV with Eldridge, Count Basie, Billie Holiday, Jimmy Rushing, Thelonious Monk, Coleman Hawkins, Ben Webster, Rex Stewart, Red Allen, and other luminaries. During the rehearsals and blocking sessions, Roy played with every bit of his astonishing energy. He not only wanted to keep on top of everybody else on the set but also, as he put it, "I can never say all I want to say." So he kept trying to.

The most accurate description of Roy's playing was by Roy himself: "I love to hear a note cracking. A real snap. It's like a whip when it happens. It hits hard and it's really clean, round and cracked."

Roy came out of Pittsburgh and as a boy didn't bother to learn to read music because anything he heard, he could play. When he was fifteen, however, in a band with other boys who couldn't read, he learned the price of ignorance. Hired for a show, the apprentice musicians found stands with manuscript paper in front of them.

"The curtain went up," Eldridge told me, "and the audience saw us crying."

"What happened then?" I asked.

"The curtain went down."

Eldridge learned how to read music on the road. He played with territory bands and big New York–based bands and intermittently headed his own, intensely driving combos. Featured with Gene Krupa and Artie Shaw, he found that Jim Crow was a constant traveling companion, especially for a black musician in a white band.

"I went to a place where we were supposed to play a dance, and they wouldn't even let me in," he recalled. "'This is a white dance,' they said. And there was my name right outside—Roy 'Little Jazz' Eldridge—and I told them who I was. When I finally did get in, I played that first set, trying to keep from crying. By the time I got through the set, the tears were rolling down my cheeks."

Artie Shaw got the gatekeeper fired, but Eldridge told himself, "Never again!"

He often played afterward in integrated settings, but they were either in Europe, New York clubs, or under the fierce aegis of Granz, who would cancel a concert rather than make even the slightest compromise with segregation.

Eldrige made some of his most compelling records for Granz, and one, *Count Basie & Roy Eldridge: Loose Walk* (Pablo), was recorded in 1972 in West Germany. The session has such vivid storytellers as tenor saxophonist Eddie "Lockjaw" Davis and trombonist Al Grey. Eldridge is intimately lyrical on "I Surrender Dear" and sounds like a whip on the other tracks. The spare, laid-back Basie is moved by these bold pilgrims to break out into some robust two-handed stride piano that hadn't been heard much from him in years.

In 1980 Eldridge had a heart attack. When he recovered, he might have been able to resume trumpet playing—if he had been anyone but Roy Eldridge. But his doctor knew it would be impossible for Roy to play the horn noncompetitively. Even if he was just practicing by himself, Roy would be going for the high notes.

So the trumpet remained in its case. Eldridge, however, has played gigs as a singer. (He's a pungent conjugator of the blues as well as a nifty rhythm vocalist.) He also can play piano and drums and is a notably candid panelist at jazz gatherings. For some years, Eldridge also was in demand as a pied piper in schools, encouraging the kids to take up instruments and study music—playing and *reading* it.

Toward the end, Eldridge made very few appearances because his wife, Vi, was ill and required nearly constant care. But he still hoped to finish his autobiography, which he'd been working on since at least 1950. His problem was with publishers and the writers they sent to assist him.

"There's a lot of stuff that should be told," Roy, at seventy-seven, told me. "But some of it they don't want me to say. And some of what they want to put in, I don't want to say."

It could have been a powerful book, like the life that went into it. And as Roy said, "There are few of us left out there." He was indeed one of the last of the originals of classic jazz. I saw him at a party a few months before his death. He was playing exultant stride piano, and he still seemed to me larger than life.

THE LEGENDARY BIG NICK

Musicians used to tell of the jazz horn men who would ride into town and, without need of a microphone, fill a nightclub or dance hall, and the streets outside, with their huge sound. On tenor saxophone, for instance, there were Coleman Hawkins, Ben Webster, and Don Byas—men who carried their horns as if they were going into battle. Few of those with such vibrant fullness of sound and color are left, and many of those few are in their autumnal years—though they play with no less fire than the younger jazzmen. Some of the latter, though, are more interested in how much and how fast they can play than in how it sounds.

In June 1983, during a night of tribute to Coleman Hawkins at the Kool Jazz Festival in New York, several saxophonists of robust vintage appeared, but the one who most intrigued both the musicians and the more knowing members of the audience was a large man with huge hands who holds his horn out from his body at a forty-five-degree angle—so he can control his breathing more easily. George Walker "Big Nick" Nicholas, radiating his pleasure at being in the limelight after so long a time in limbo, resounded throughout Avery Fisher Hall. He had a mike, but he didn't need it.

Most members of the audience were hearing Big Nick for the

first time because for the past twenty-five years his club appearances in New York have been infrequent. His leisurely, romantic style has not been in vogue, although there were signs—including bookings in such Manhattan clubs as Fat Tuesday's—that, as he says, the wheel is turning in his direction again. "To the real thing," he explains.

Musicians, in any case, have always kept Nick in mind. John Coltrane used to urge me to go to Brooklyn or wherever Nick had a short gig, to hear "that sound, that control." John Coltrane, the lodestar of all jazz musicians after him, named a song for his older friend. The title was "Big Nick." Dizzy Gillespie, in whose band Nick played in 1948, was another fan.

There is a warmth in this survivor—a presence, a reminder of the time when all those big men seemed to fill the air all around with their roars, whoops, cries, shouts, and urgent love calls.

Big Nick comes from Saginaw, Michigan, where, he notes, his father became "the first Negro in the state to work for the Bell telephone system. He was a handyman." In 1941, when he was nineteen years old, Nick, encouraged by his father, hit the road—serving apprenticeships with Earl Hines, Tiny Bradshaw, Claude Hopkins, and Dizzy Gillespie, among others. From 1950 to 1952, Nick had the kind of a job a genie might have gotten him—talent booker, master of ceremonies, and leader of the band at the Paradise Club in Harlem. Members of the jazz royalty, from Coleman Hawkins to Billie Holiday, often came by. ("What do you want to sing, baby?" Nick would ask Lady Day. She would look up at him and say, "I just came to listen to you.")

Langston Hughes was a regular, along with actors William Marshall and James Edwards. And on the stand there usually was some kind of sound of surprise, because Nick would hire such then "controversial" originals as Thelonious Monk and Betty Carter. When business was slow, he'd take his horn out into the street and those big, mellow sounds would surround bemused passersby and gentle them into the club.

After the Paradise became a memory, Nick took whatever gigs he could find. Some of them, in far-flung cities, were engagements as a "single." He would come in alone, and hometown rhythm sections hired by the local innkeeper would then provide Nick with what might euphemistically be called "a challenge." He would have been able to bring his own sidemen and still come out with more money, if he'd had some records out. But no one had ever asked him to make an album as a leader. Back in the Paradise Club nights, Charlie Parker, after learning a number of tunes from Big Nick, asked him, "Do you mind if I take these downtown and record them?"

"No, I don't mind," Nick said wistfully. "They don't let me record, so you go ahead and do those tunes."

At last, however, Big Nick Nicholas has an album of his own: *Big and Warm* (India Navigation). Jazz aficionado Bob Cummins, who owns the label, produces only what he likes, and having caught a couple of Big Nick club dates, Mr. Cummins made the phone call that Nick thought would never come.

"My first album in forty years and four months," he said recently with a satisfaction he didn't bother to contain. "But you know, there are so many people who haven't gotten that far. I know many musicians who play so beautifully they would take your breath away. But they never left their hometowns. They had a house, they had children, they had a job four or five nights a week. They weren't going to give that up. So they never came to New York, and they never had a recording. I consider myself fortunate."

Nick's debut album includes—along with the big, round, thrusting sound of his tenor saxophone—three of his vocals. Sounding like a deep-voiced walrus in love for the first time, Nicholas has a distinctively appealing style on that instrument too. Among the tunes in the set are "Autumn in New York," "I'm All Smiles," and "Georgia." I could see Billie Holiday at the Paradise Club, listening, smiling slightly.

Of the four-man rhythm section, two are young members of whiz-kid trumpeter Wynton Marsalis's combo: bassist Phil Bowler and drummer Jeff Watts. Like Coleman Hawkins used to, Big Nick listens closely to newcomers. "Now, these two fellows," he told me, "have listened to older musicians. You can hear it in them."

And Nicholas has been noticing that there are more younger listeners in the jazz clubs these nights. "Some of them," he says, "are beginning to realize that they were raised on jazz music. They hear something and they say, 'Oh, my father used to play a record of that at home.' They're getting that nostalgic feeling, and there's nothing more powerful than that."

He is at last optimistic that the young, or some of them, may focus more on sound. "I mean a sound that comes from real feeling," he says. "From a musician who is telling a story. I was always a sound man. I listened to Coleman Hawkins, and then I found out that Coleman listened to Pablo Casals. So I started listening to Pablo Casals. Then I listened to the complete Duke Ellington sound and Billie Holiday and Mahalia Jackson. When I was coming up, there were people who didn't have to know what key a song was in. They could tell by your sound if they wanted to listen to you play that song."

Big Nick expects more club dates to come in as a result of his new album. Meanwhile, he keeps leading the improvised life of a musician who waits for the phone to tell him his future. Nick has no regrets, having lived most of his years that way. And the album, of course, will not change his way of living.

"I'm still doing the same thing," Big Nick says, laughing. "Trying to get somewhere."

THE MAN WHO BECAME HIS HORN

On listening to a younger player with prodigious technique, Lester Young, a jazzman of subtle elegance, would sometimes ask him: "What's your story?" What are you saying?

He never asked that of Ruby Braff, the most lyrical cornetist in jazz since Louis Armstrong and Bobby Hackett. As with them, each of his solos is indeed a story—a highly personal variation on memories and desires unearthed by the particular tune he's playing by Gershwin, Johnny Mercer, Rodgers and Hart, or others in the large repertory of classic American songs he has in his head. Mr. Braff abhors excessive notes, and as Alec Wilder said, every note he does play "is the center of that note."

I have known Ruby Braff since he was twelve years old and already working gigs in Boston, and I have never known anyone more stubborn. From the beginning, he would listen only to such true originals as Louis Armstrong, Billie Holiday, and Lester Young. And he would play only himself, as that musical self was being gradually shaped by his mentors on recordings.

Classic jazz, with plenty of melody that was not to be bruised by the improviser, began to go out of fashion in the 1950s, as bop, with its fragmented melodies and dizzying rhythms and harmonies, took over much of the jazz scene. Then came cool jazz, in which the overt joy of a Louis Armstrong was considered quite gross by some musicians. Mr. Braff made no concessions to these new enthusiasms among critics, performers, and audiences and kept playing what, to him, is the only right stuff.

Over the years he found an audience that has kept on growing—listeners who like the kind of jazz that makes them feel good, the way Louis Armstrong and Count Basie did; music that flows deep and easy as it swings; and sounds that are full, round, and glowing with the pulse of life.

As Derek Jewell has noted of Mr. Braff in the *London Times*, "The richest gold is his soft playing in the lower register, the sternest test of lip and control, where much more fashionable players fluff and mumble like men with their feet in mud."

A characteristic Braff recording, *A Sailboat in the Moonlight* (Concord), pairs him on the front line with tenor saxophonist Scott Hamilton. Twenty-seven years younger than the sixty-four-year-old Mr. Braff, Mr. Hamilton is equally devoted to classical jazz and the delights of melodic variation. Together they play songs not likely to be heard on any other jazz album of the year: the title tune, "When Lights Are Low," "Sweethearts on Parade," and "Where Are You?" Both are singing horns and both can be sweet and lowdown at the same time.

There is a naturalness in Mr. Braff's playing—it is as if he is conversing through his horn—that has been there since I first heard it. I was fourteen, practicing the clarinet alongside an open window in the Roxbury section of Boston. While I could play anything I could read, improvising was a mystery to me. Suddenly, I heard a peremptory bark from the street.

"Hey, kid! You want to come to a session? The arrangements aren't hard."

Down below was a short, impatient twelve-year-old, Ruby Braff. I trotted along, started to play the charts, and then, piercing through the paper and my very soul was a soaring horn, lovingly stretching and turning and caressing the melody so authoritatively that I knew right then that I would never be a jazz musician but that I surely was in the presence of one.

When he's not playing, Mr. Braff is sometimes, to use a euphemism, argumentative. Indeed, a few years ago, in certain jazz circles, T-shirts appeared bearing the message I HAD A BEEF

WITH RUBY BRAFF. But once he begins to play, Mr. Braff resembles Louis Armstrong in the clarity of his priorities. Armstrong once said, "When I pick up that horn . . . that's my living and my life. I love them notes. That's why I try to make them right. . . . I don't want a million dollars. See what I mean? There's no medals. I mean, you got to live with that horn."

Rudy Braff is one of those players who is his horn, and that total absorption gives him a powerful musical presence. When he leads a small combo, he transforms the musicians in it. Scott Hamilton describes gigs in which Mr. Braff was a guest leader: "He'd get in front of bands that would be playing together for years, and from the very first note, the character of the band would be different. . . . [With Ruby] the guys have to pay a lot more attention than they are used to doing, and sometimes that draws performances out of musicians that you wouldn't ordinarily get."

He also draws the unexpected out of songs. In *America the Beautiful* (Concord), the only instrument besides Mr. Braff's cornet is a pipe organ (Dick Hyman); during that spacious program, he engages in a rhapsodic jazz illumination of "America the Beautiful" that is heartfelt, respectfully hip, and unique in the annals of jazz.

The uncompromising Mr. Braff, recently reflecting in the third person on his career, observes with justified pride that "Braff has appeared on many TV shows, as well as at the most prestigious festivals. He now plays on both sides of the Atlantic and has recorded with every major record label in the world."

What may have pleased him most, however, was a vote cast in a poll of musicians in the 1956 *Encyclopedia of Jazz* yearbook. Voting for "New Star" on trumpet, Louis Armstrong chose Ruby Braff. As a boy, Ruby was drawn to his life's work by hearing, as he recalls, Louis Armstrong's "big orange tone."

A few years ago, a young trumpeter listening to Mr. Braff at a club said, "The guy has an incredible respect for himself, and it shows in his music." It also accounts for his survival.

PART VI
listening ahead

IS THERE A CHARLIE PARKER
AMONG THE NEW GENERATION
OF JAZZ PLAYERS?

About twenty years ago I began to think jazz was dying. Many of the young players were increasingly immersed in "free jazz"—where melody, swing, or harmony were at best accidental, and fleeting. While some of those players were earnest experimenters, others were hustlers. If some didn't know how to swing, for instance, no one listening to free jazz could tell.

Others of the young were seduced by "fusion," a lumpy mixture of jazz and rock. Much of the integrity remaining among youthful improvisers rested in the apprentice boppers, carrying on the tradition of Charlie Parker, Dizzy Gillespie, and the other blazing modernists who revolutionized jazz in the forties. But too many of these acolytes sounded like recordings of the past even when they were playing live.

The day I was almost sure jazz might have no future was when I picked up an album by reed man Anthony Braxton, acclaimed by the inner insiders as a key shaper of the jazz to come. The liner notes, written by Braxton, consisted largely of mathematical equations. Count Basie's definition of jazz was "music you can pat your foot to." He didn't say anything about needing a protractor.

The music inside the Braxton album was indeed meticulously designed but was otherwise empty.

During the past few years, however, there has been an astonishing change in direction among the newest wave of young improvisers. Players in their early twenties, some in their teens, are sounding as if they have roots way back in jazz.

Wycliffe Gordon, in his early twenties and, at the time, a trombonist with Wynton Marsalis's band, told the *New York Times* how his life was changed when he was twelve. He heard an early Louis Armstrong recording, "Keyhole Blues." It was in a five-volume history of jazz that his great-aunt left behind when she died. Says Gordon: "The instruments expressed themselves vocally, as if they were singing, instead of just playing those little mechanical cliches that funk and rock musicians have been using."

For those youngsters who did not have so hip a great-aunt, Wynton Marsalis is, as one of the players puts it, "the shepherd" of these celebrators of the whole jazz heritage. Marsalis has been disseminating the true faith ever since he became well-enough known to be listened to.

And the fact that he has been financially successful without commercializing his music has impressed young jazz makers around the country. Virtue, they see, brings more than its own reward. Wynton Marsalis is so intent on keeping to pure jazz that he fired his brother, saxophonist Branford Marsalis, for going on tour with the rock singer Sting. Somewhat complicating this particular morality play is that Branford is a more spontaneous and passionate jazz improviser than his brother.

In recent years, Wynton Marsalis has made it a point, during his tours, to visit schools and jazz workshops. There he speaks compellingly of the legacy and challenge of black jazz; and he also befriends, counsels, and stays in touch with musicians of particular promise. Many of those now recording albums of their own are protégés of this itinerant preacher of the jazz gospel. Others know of him, have heard his recordings, and have been converted.

Among the young who are rescuing jazz from losing its identity are trumpeters Roy Hargrove and Marlon Jordan. These leaders and their colleagues swing crisply, gently illuminate ballads, and play with attention to how they sound. Instead of the squawks, barks, and howls that have characterized some free jazz, these musicians have a fullness and depth of sound that recall the jazz players of the swing era who disdained a thin, raw way of identifying themselves.

Among others in the new second line are pianist Geoff Keezer; trumpeter Nicholas Payton; trombonist/record producer Delfeayo Marsalis; guitarist Mark Whitfield; tenor saxophonist Joshua Redman; and alto saxophonist Antonio Hart. The list of young comers is much longer, and there are already players in their early teens who are ready to challenge their immediate elders.

In the jazz community as a whole, there is not unadulterated joy over the sudden attention being given to players of an age once thought right for apprentices. Some of the musicians in their forties and fifties are finding it hard to get record dates since the companies see more sales potential in these proficient youngsters who are getting much more press than, say, such seasoned and continually brilliant jazzmen as bassist Ron Carter and drummer Roy Haynes.

"At 19, 20," Carter tells *Time* magazine, "how much can you know?" On the other hand, how much did Louis Armstrong, Coleman Hawkins, and Lester Young know when they started as striplings? But—the rebuttal to that goes—they started as learners. They didn't have their own albums so soon.

And Dizzy Gillespie, who has the most generous spirit in all of jazz, can't keep himself from saying to me about this bustling crop, "You don't see no Charlie Parkers coming along."

Not yet. And maybe the next Parker or John Coltrane will come from somewhere far away—like Siberia—where the jazz is hot and unpredictable. But whatever happens, these serious young men here, who can also spread joy, have shown the way to even younger players. A way that has no need for mathematical diagrams in liner notes.

Still, there is some disquiet about the future. Alto saxophonist Benny Carter, in his eighties and always immediately identifiable, says of the new breed, "They can play anything. But often, I can't tell one from the other."

CAN WYNTON MARSALIS
LEARN TO LAUGH?

When I was a child, my music teacher told me I could best learn the names of the notes on the lines of the staff by keeping in mind that Every Good Boy Does Fine. After all these years, I am finally able to visualize that paragon of exemplary musical behavior climbing up the staff. He is Wynton Marsalis, who may be the most self-disciplined jazzman in the history of that volcanic art.

Indeed, Marsalis has discipline to spare, having become so accomplished at classical music that in 1984 he won Grammy awards for both his jazz and classical recordings. And when he takes time out from practicing and composing, he does not let his mind slow down. Marsalis told a *Los Angeles Times* interviewer last year that he was reading four books at once: Ralph Ellison's *Going to the Country*, John Chernoff's *African Rhythm and African Sensibility*, C. A. Diop's *Cultural Unity of Black Africa*, and Thomas Mann's *Doctor Faustus*.

In a club or concert hall, Marsalis invariably wears impressively subdued, expensive suits and ties. ("I think serious musicians shouldn't look like they're playing street football.") He is also the author of an exceptionally compelling plea that the jazz heritage be taken seriously, especially by the people from whom it originally came. In "Why We Must Preserve Our Jazz Heritage," which appeared in *Ebony* in 1986, Marsalis declared: "Jazz is something Negroes invented and it said the most profound things not only about us and the way we look at things, but about what modern democratic life is really about . . . Jazz has all of the elements, from the spare and penetrating to the complex and enveloping. It is the hardest music to play that I know of and it is the highest rendition of individual emotion in the history of Western music."

Marsalis brings that message to schools, as when he once directed six young black trumpeters and saxophonists in a classroom in the South Bronx. To kids who were slouching, Marsalis said, "Sit erect, with some style and some pride." He smiled. "Lift your horn with some dignity."

A son and student of Ellis Marsalis, a pianist and fabled teacher in New Orleans, Wynton has been serious about his horn since he was twelve. Five years later he was doing very fine, both at jazz and at the Berkshire Music Center at Tanglewood where he was chosen an outstanding brass player. Then came Juilliard, after which Marsalis acquired a strenuous postgraduate education in improvising while with Art Blakey's Jazz Messengers. Blakey makes the drums sound and feel like an onrushing forest fire, a dangerous ambiance for which Juilliard is not able to prepare even its very best students. Marsalis survived coolly.

In recent years, with the proceeds from his sturdily selling Columbia LPs and performance dates in this country and abroad, Marsalis has made enough money to endow scholarships at various schools, and he plays a lot of benefit concerts. In every way he is, as he intends to be, a role model for young black musicians. Not only with regard to self-discipline but also on matters of musical integrity. He has no patience, for instance, with attempts to fuse rock music and jazz.

Wynton Marsalis's music is undiluted jazz. The sound (or rather, sounds) of his trumpet are never "brassy" or clattering. Mostly mellow and singing, his lines are unfailingly clear, cohesive, and subtly surprising. That is, you think you know where they're going, but somehow they've circled around behind you. And he swings, fluidly, like a bicyclist riding with his hands in his pockets.

And yet, something's missing. I didn't have quite the word for what isn't there until I heard a concert at the JVC Jazz Festival in New York. It was called "Wynton Marsalis Salutes Dizzy Gillespie on His Seventieth Birthday." Marsalis wore a white suit that made Thomas Wolfe's seem in memory to be rather baggy. In honor of Dizzy, Marsalis opened the evening with a series of Dizzy's demanding compositions, which he executed with aplomb. Marsalis also introduced one of his own pieces, "The Source," dedicated to Gillespie. Between numbers Wynton spoke at some moralizing length, telling us at one point, in reference to Dizzy's works, that "we all know civilization is an act of will. Things we enjoy come from an act of human effort."

At intermission, I went upstairs to Dizzy's dressing room with Jonah Jones, an often luminous trumpet player and an admirer of Louis Armstrong and Dizzy.

"You know," Dizzy said of Marsalis, "he told me last night that he's studying all my records. He's getting them from collectors. And when he's done, he says, there'll be nothing of mine that he's missing. He'll know why I sound like I do."

Dizzy smiled in appreciation of such diligence. "Of course," he added, "how definite a style he will create for himself, from all he knows—that's something else. But there's no reason it won't come."

"Can he study how to bring joy into his playing?" I asked Dizzy. "That's what's missing."

Dizzy laughed heartily and said nothing.

"That's age," said Jones. "He hasn't experienced enough."

When the concert continued, Dizzy, exuding delight, appeared in a tieless though festive shirt and a shapeless pair of pants. Just about everything he played made you feel good, and even the pauses between notes were alive with the excitement to come. In one number, the four-man trumpet section—pausing while Dizzy, in a cadenza, celebrated all those years of being Dizzy—laughed out loud in pleasure.

I suppose it is possible to learn joy. But I remember Clifford Brown and others who had it when they were younger than Wynton. Well, Wynton says, "I'm not even close to what I'm gonna be." He is clearly capable of unstinting effort. But, I asked Dizzy, "have you ever seen Wynton laugh?" Dizzy laughed at the unlikelihood of that sight.

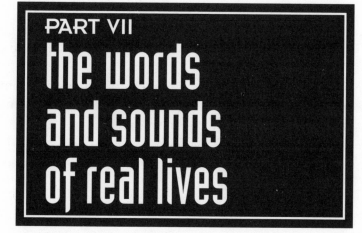

PART VII

the words and sounds of real lives

MY LIFE IN COUNTRY MUSIC

Around three o'clock in the morning, the Lester Flatt-Earl Scruggs bus pulled into a truckstop outside Huntsville, Alabama. In awful need of a beer, I was first off. At the counter, several good old boys nudged each other. In 1962, down there, a beard, especially attached to a face that could have come from no kin of theirs, was like a door prize. They crowded around me, making mean small talk that could have only one end.

Behind me came the banjo player, face closed as always, and he lightly put his arm on my shoulder, not saying anything. The good old boys were mighty impressed at this visitation, forgetting the alien. "How do you do it so fast, Earl?" one of them asked him. And he showed them the lightning Scruggs three-finger style—in the air.

Back in the bus, on the way to Tennessee, Uncle Josh Graves, the dobro man, was laughing. "I hope you learned something," he told me. "Stick with the musicians, and you'll come out all right."

Well, I'd been knowing that for a long time, except that up to then, the musicians I'd known had been mostly black. I had heard a lot of white country sounds; one hour a day for nine years in Boston radio, I had to play, in arrogant ignorance, Kitty

Wells, Ernest Tubb, Hank Snow, and other such strangers. None of them stayed in my mind. Except Jimmie Rodgers, "the Singing Brakeman," because I heard some black in him.

Later, in New York, after the last set at Birdland, I'd catch southern radio stations and did not turn them off.

So, in time, I went down to Nashville and first got to know Earl Scruggs. His musical stories, of course, have roots in centuries of dancing and drinking on the old-country island. "There's Irish in there," I said one afternoon when Scruggs took a banjo from under his bed and gently twanged a song from his boyhood.

"A lot more than Irish," said the man from Flint Hill, North Carolina. "There's black in there, too. No musician with ears can leave out the black."

For long stretches on the bus, Earl would not talk at all. It was like spending daydreaming time with Thelonious Monk. "I'm going to appear at one of those antiwar rallies," Scruggs once broke a silence. "They tell me not to or Martha *White Flour* might drop us. People in towns like Huntsville, Alabama, might drop us. But that's what I'm going to do."

"How could you stand being with nothing but crackers?" a hipster New York friend asked me when I came back from time on the road with Earl Scruggs.

Years later, I got to know another country musicianer, as Sidney Bechet would say. Maybe the saddest man I've ever known. But back then, on the right night, listening to him was like hearing Beethoven metamorphosed into a funky saloon singer and barrelhouse pianist. Such hugeness of feeling, especially loneliness, but controlled by a beat so hard and driving that pity would turn into the exhilaration of music triumphant. And some of the numbers were straight-out roaring blues. He was the Silver Fox, Charlie Rich, with the long white mane of a professional wrestler, the face of a professional drinker, and the eyes of an amateur at knowing why he was here.

Charlie, a boy from a farm near Colt, Arkansas, had also heard black in the air, as well as white country sounds, and his obsession was jazz. When I knew him, the recordings Charlie listened to at home were those of Miles Davis and Count Basie.

But long before, in his own music, the Silver Fox had taken another route. And even if he could find that junction again—and he'd thought about looking—he'd have to pass it by once more. Charlie had paid far too much dues in scores of gin mills where Miles's presence would have cleared the room. And now—this was about 1973—it looked as if all those hoarse nights were going to pay off. Charlie's records were pole-vaulting up the country-music charts, and television producers were making urgent noises.

The Silver Fox was part terrified and part lustful at his imminent ascension. "They say," he told me one night, "that I'm not supposed to play the piano much anymore. I got to sing standing up so I can be seen and so I can move around, saying things between songs. They hired somebody to write out those things. It won't seem right without the piano, but I see their point."

Charlie did indeed hit big. He wasn't singing "Don't Put No Tombstone on My Grave" anymore. Nor was he able to improvise on the piano, one of his great pleasures in the past. And his manager had him taking dancing lessons so the Silver Fox could move more gracefully through his newly choreographed act. But Charlie now had his own airplane, *The Silver Fox,* and three young black women as backup singers.

Toward the end of 1975, during a network telecast of the Country Music Association Awards, Charlie was scheduled to open an envelope that would reveal the name of the Entertainer of the Year. The Silver Fox was "fairly plowed," as an onlooker told me. He took the envelope, opened it, looked at the slip, got a cigarette lighter out of his pocket, and burned the envelope in front of all country-music-loving America. "John Denver!" Charlie then announced the winner to an aghast assembly.

There were various explanations for this understandable burning, as some who have heard John Denver will agree. One tale was that Charlie, thinking he had been bitten by a snake, was on medication which, along with a taste of the booze, befuddled his sense of the fitting. An astute country-music journalist on the scene told me, however, "In bibulousness there is honesty, especially with Charlie." In any case, after this historic act of symbolic music criticism, Charlie's career has been somewhat flattened.

The plane is gone, as are the black backup singers; and Charlie, down to an unchoreographed quartet, is playing more piano now. He still hits Las Vegas and Lake Tahoe, so there's no present danger of a return to the gin mills. The Silver Fox is also back to playing more blues, so things may be looking up.

Shortly after I checked on the Silver Fox, I told a reporter friend that James Talley, who is his own kind of country singer, was coming to the Lone Star Cafe in the Village for just one night.

"Well," she said, "I'm not into country music. It all sounds pretty much the same. Can't tell one of them from another. And it has no soul."

WHITE LINE FEVER

It is a game played by children of all ages. Depending on the alleged sophistication of the participants, the creepy questions can range from "Which would you rather lose, an arm or a leg?" to "Which would you rather be—impotent for the rest of your life or the Elephant Man?" (Ah, but who knows what horny compassion lurks in all manner of sensitive women?) The most common version is: "If you had to choose between being blind and deaf, which would it be?"

I played the game in elementary school, and I played it a couple of months ago, when I answered without hesitation: "Blind." There was hooting incredulity. I am so compulsive a reader that I read while walking in the street, including at night, by flashlight. Nonetheless, I tried to explain, for me music is a much, much deeper need. Like, if I have to go without it for a few days, I get to feeling hollow. But I can go for weeks without reading the First Amendment.

The reason this comes to mind has to do with my being at the bar of the Lone Star Cafe on lower Fifth Avenue one late afternoon in 1980. On the stand, going through a sound test and a lighting test, were Merle Haggard and the Strangers, ten weathered-looking klezmorim of quite varied ages. They'd been playing together so long that they were swinging with powerfully relaxed ease from note one. In the front line, a tall, bearded, impassive man in his early middle years took a swig from a bottle of beer, picked up an alto saxophone, and cut through the band, cut through the years, with a lean, hot, jumping solo that brought Pete Brown, Don Stovall, and other startling jazz ghosts into my head. I hadn't felt so satisfied in a long time.

But this was a white cat, Don Markham of Bakersfield, California, and this was a country band. Yeah, but there's a hell of a lot more to country than most trendy city folk think. Especially with Haggard and his obsession with roots, all kinds of roots. There's nobody playing country now who *knows* as much as Haggard. He's a practicing expert on Jimmie Rodgers, Bob Wills's western swing, Lefty Frizzell, and Hank Williams. And Haggard himself is, except for Bill Monroe, the only singer/musician/writer left whose own body of work makes him fit right into that company of lasting originals. It's like Kris Kristofferson said a couple of years ago: "When we speak of Haggard, we aren't speaking about how he's going to come out on the Country Music Association Awards this year; we're talking about posterity."

At that moment in the Lone Star, however, Haggard was very much into the present. He started going over some songs he must have played hundreds of times, but he wasn't satisfied. As it used to be in Duke Ellington's band, Haggard's arrangements are constantly subject to editing. Wearing a railroad cap, jeans, workshirt, a white nylon windbreaker, and western boots, the wiry Okie was tinkering with the tempo of "I'm a Lonesome Fugitive," a song that is not his but that years ago, he says, "gave me a direction for writing. I mean, it was a true song." It was then he decided he could write about his own true life, including his time in prison. If it hadn't been for "Fugitive," he might have tried to hide his past, which, to his astonishment, turned out to be "one of the most interesting things about me."

Haggard, with as much controlled intensity as if he were playing to a packed room rather than to us strays at the bar, started "Fugitive" again ("Down every road there's always one more city/I'm on the run, the highway is my home"). Lead guitarist Roy Nichols—no household name but revered by guitarists all over the world—lined out a biting, crackling commentary. But suddenly Haggard gestured it all into silence and worked for a while with the band on getting different guitar/violin/horn voicings. "And," he looked up at one of his two drummers, "not so strong. It's got to be lighter."

The one woman on the stand, Bonnie Owens, stepped off and came over to the bar, where I cleared a seat for her by removing various newspapers of mine that had no business being there anyway. She has reddish-brown hair and an extraordinarily clear, open look. Introducing herself rather diffidently as "the harmony singer with Merle Haggard," she insisted on buying me a beer for my courtesy; and as the musicians moved into another song, Bonnie said, "We have the best band in the country, you know." And paused. "The best singer too."

I agreed, adding that I have all of Haggard's albums.

She was surprised hearing this from someone who was manifestly not a good old boy. A good old Yossele Rosenblatt boy, maybe, but where does this stranger come to "White Line Fever"? "I know a lot of people," Bonnie told me, "who would *kill* for all his albums."

Bonnie, now forty-eight but looking some ten years younger, used to be more than a harmony singer. In the midsixties, while featured with her then-husband, Merle Haggard, she won the Academy of Country & Western Music's Top Female Vocalist award. But she spent more and more of her energy taking care of Merle's business and even retired from performing in 1975. For a while. I'd last seen her several years ago, in an auditorium. By then Bonnie was one of several backup singers for Haggard. That night she was banging a tambourine as well and having one hell of a problem keeping it and herself in time. Merle finally came over to her and in front of all those people, took the tambourine, and plopped it on her head. He didn't seem to be funning.

They were divorced a couple of years ago, and when Merle remarried, Bonnie was the bridesmaid. (If you want to read about how that happened, look at Peter Guralnick's chapter on Merle in his indispensable book *Lost Highway*, published by Godine. It's as if Chekhov had filed a report from Harrah's in Lake Tahoe.)

Bonnie stayed with the band and is now the *only* harmony singer. Everybody in the entourage says that Bonnie is Merle's best friend. Merle says that too. So how do you figure that? You usually divorce someone you can't stand. Merle's answer is that Aries people are not easy to live with. Bonnie also got into his repertory. He wrote "I Can't Be What You Want Me to Be" for her. The subsequent Haggard marriage, I was told, is not in what you'd call a mellow groove. "She's a real ballbreaker," someone says of Bonnie's successor.

Haggard waves for Bonnie to go back on the stand. The spots, red and blue, are on, and outside, although it's not yet six, people are lining up for Merle's first show—four hours from now. Some have been there since two o'clock in the afternoon.

This is the first club date Haggard has ever played in New York. "I got nothing at all against this man's place in here," Haggard tells me, "but it's kind of cramped." And Bonnie had said, "He loves being closer to the people so he can find out what they want and what they're living like. But," she smiled to indicate she meant no offense, "we've never played in a club this small."

Haggard agreed to the one-night booking because there was a syndicated "live" radio show out of the Lone Star that covers much of the country. Also, word had been getting out to even the most renowned and picky country performers that the Lone Star was a good club to work. You get your money. All of it. And a lot of exposure. It took Mort Cooperman, the musical architect of the Lone Star, a while to break down some of the southern suspicion of Yankee traders and particularly of Jewish-Yankee entrepreneurs. But he's done it. Why, not long ago, in the middle of a negotiating conversation on the phone with a country power in Nashville, Cooperman said, "Hey, I'm the one who's supposed to be the Jew." That old southern boy laughed and laughed.

The band is really cooking. On a ballad, the fiddle player is spinning so sensuous a solo that I remember Peter Rowan—describing a mountain player whose "harmonies glowed in the dark." Haggard, rocking slightly on his heels, is smiling, and one of the guitarists is so taken with the good feeling in the air that he grins at me, one music-loving stranger to another.

Later that night, too, members of the band had plenty of solo space. Haggard has no patience with the commercial country framework in which the musicians are just there to wait on the soloist. As he recently said to a *Down Beat* reporter, "If I can't feature the instrumentalists, I just don't want to be in the business."

He digs the sounds around him so much that not long ago, when his present wife, Leona Williams, wanted to give him a surprise birthday party in a remote Florida nightclub, she arranged to have the whole band come down there that evening because she knew that's what Merle most wanted to hear, night off or not.

It is just past six at the Lone Star, and Merle calls "White Line Fever." Drawing out the first two words as if he were actually tracing lines on the highway, Haggard—in that firm, slightly gritty, blues-touched voice—sings:

The years keep flying by like the high line poles
The wrinkles in my forehead show the miles I've put
 behind me
They continue to remind me how fast I'm growing old
Guess I'll die with this fever in my soul.

Hypnotically, in the failing light, the refrain of wh-i-i-i-te l-i-i-i-ne fever, medium-slow, with Roy Nichols's guitar keening into the far distance, immobilizes us all as Haggard comes up to the mike again, with Bonnie harmonizing on the side: "Yeah, I've been from coast to coast a hundred times or more/I ain't seen one single place where I ain't been before."

The musicians began to leave, and the Nashville publicity man came over to tell me he still didn't know if Haggard would agree to be interviewed. "He's a very private man," he said. Everybody tells me Haggard's a very private man. Bonnie said it too. "He told me no press in New York," the nervous but amiable young man went on, "but maybe he'll make a couple of exceptions."

Usually, unless I'm on a muckraking kind of story, if someone insists on being that private, I leave him to himself. The golden rule, you know. But I'm very curious about Haggard, and I don't have that many live musical heroes anymore. So I stick around. And it pays off. Haggard was not at all reticent about talking. He turns out, by the way, to be so knowledgeable about jazz that he cited—as an influence on the legendary country singer Jimmie Rodgers—a pop jazz singer out of the twenties, Emmett Miller, whom I'd never heard of. I didn't tell Haggard that I had to look Miller up afterward.

Later that night, about halfway through Haggard's first set, he introduced to the happily cramped crowd "My favorite girl singer—Bonnie Owens! She's been with us for fifteen years. And she's going to do us a song she wrote."

Bonnie, smiling, said, "I wrote this song, 'I'll Be What I Want to Be,' for all the women in New York. But," she added quickly, "it's not a women's lib song."

"You wouldn't have much of a chance with it if it was," Haggard said into the mike with somewhat excessive good humor. "Not with all the male chauvinist pigs on *this* stage."

With the band rolling behind her, Bonnie, in a crisp, pungent, pleasant voice, ran the changes on independence. "I ain't gonna do nothing I don't want to do never again!" She ended, with hands triumphantly raised, "I like *me!*"

Merle Haggard looked very proud. Later on he went into a song of his about a man whose wife had split and left him to bring up the kids. Listening, I wondered if there are any children in rock songs—aside from the children, of whatever age, doing the singing.

Toward the end there was another kind of what Jimmy Rushing used to call a he/she song. ("The foundation of all song," Rushing said.) Merle went into "Today I Started Loving You Again/And I'm Right Back Where I've Always Been." There's nobody in country music or anywhere else who can sing as tenderly as Haggard. The sound, the feeling, he gets talking to a woman are like what Michael Harper wrote for Bud Powell: "there's no rain anywhere, soft enough for you."

But then, an explosion of the blues, "Trouble in Mind," in which Haggard and the Strangers emblazoned on our very souls a fiery, exultant tribute to all the blues singers and players they have known—black, white, city, country, dead, and alive. When it was over, Haggard sighed in satisfaction: "Oh, I feel *good!*"

"You know," he had told me earlier, "this may sound corny, but when it looks like everything else is breaking up in the country and in the world, and in your own life, I keep thinking that maybe music will be the last thing to go down."

The story is that he has a spider web tattooed on his back. "He did it when he was young and felt trapped," Bonnie Owens once told southern writer Paul Hemphill, a good listener.

Merle Haggard was the child of Okies who had been farmers near Checotah, Oklahoma, not far from Muskogee. After a disastrous fire there came a drought, and so Merle's folks (he hadn't come on the scene yet) went off to California where, as Jimmie Rodgers sang, "they sleep out every night."

James Haggard had been a pretty fair fiddler and picker back in Oklahoma; but his wife, Flossie, once her soul took fire in the Church of Christ, banned him from playing the devil's music. All the more so since their child, Merle, had been born to be reared in a straight line to the Saviour. The Haggards were living in a converted refrigerator car near Bakersfield, California, by then; and James, now a carpenter with the railroad, taught the boy fishing and hunting. But when Merle was nine, his father, as Merle later put it, abandoned him. The interviewer asked if he'd be a little more specific.

"He died," said Merle.

"Mama Tried," as Haggard later titled a song, but she failed. She could not control the boy. He ran away a lot, cut school (finally dropping out in the eighth grade), and became quite familiar to the Bakersfield police. When Merle was fourteen, Flossie put him in a juvenile home, and he escaped the next day. Merle's police record grew like Pinocchio's nose—bum checks, petty thievery, stolen cars, armed robbery. Reform schools couldn't hold him. Seven times he slid out of them. But when he and some of the boys messed up a burglary of a Bakersfield bar (they got drunk waiting for the bar to close), he got sent to a place that *could* hold him: San Quentin. He was on an indeterminate sentence of six months to fifteen and a half years.

Current conventional wisdom—from hard-liners to many reformers—is that prison can't rehabilitate anybody. But Merle, unconventional as always, insists that San Quentin turned him around. Having spent his twenty-first birthday in solitary across the hall from death row—and hearing those terminal souls trying to figure out how they'd gotten there—scared the hell out of him. "This was no movie, and I wasn't Jesse James or one of the Dalton brothers."

Haggard was in the audience when Johnny Cash came to make a recording at San Quentin, and he became part of the warden's country band. He also picked up a high school equivalency diploma. After two years and nine months, Merle Haggard was paroled; and to cut a long, hard story short, he made it very big in the music business. So now he's one happy straightened-out dude, right? Well, yes and no. ("I was born the running kind, with leaving always on my mind.")

In the band bus, as open-mouthed fans look through the window, clutching empty pages to be blessed with an autograph, we are talking about jazz and blues. I'd mentioned that one of Merle's heroes, Bob Wills, while in his teens in East Texas, used to ride fifty miles to see Bessie Smith perform.

"Sure," said Haggard. "I understand that. I go back a long way in that music myself. I go back to Louis Armstrong, Joe Venuti, Eddie Lang, Emmett Miller." (Miller, I found out when I looked him up, had a band with the Dorsey Brothers, Eddie Lang, and Jack Teagarden.)

Bonnie Owens came into the bus and soundlessly slipped into a seat diagonally across from Merle. Up front, next to where the driver would have been, nonpareil lead guitarist Roy Nichols was trying to stare some piece of electrical equipment into submission. "My big love," said Haggard, "my big jazz love was Django Reinhardt." The gypsy guitarist might have been surprised.

"What did you especially like about what he did?"

Haggard laughed. An uproarious, bus-filling laugh. "Everything."

"Yeah," Nichols filled out the chord. "Every note he played."

"And something else," Merle went on. "I understand they couldn't nail him down to record very often because he was such a free-will person. Django didn't give a shit about schedules. He just wanted to play wherever he felt like playing. That's kind of the way I am. Me and Johnny Gimble. He's that way too." (The most exultantly swinging of all country fiddlers, Gimble, a Bob Wills alumnus, is a ubiquitous session man and a headliner too.)

"Yeah," said Haggard, "Johnny doesn't give a damn *where* he plays. He just wants to be happy, have a few beers, tell jokes, and *play!*"

"You sound envious."

"You bet that's what I'd do if I could. In fact, I've started doing it some on my off-time. I can't do it when I'm working. But when

I'm off, I just sit in and play anywhere there's music. Anywhere somebody knows me and will tolerate me."

Roy Nichols snorts. "Come on, Merle."

"I've gone and sat in with Willie Nelson for five days at Harrah's." Haggard ignores his guitarist. "No money. Just for the fun of the playing." He looked past me and Bonnie into some wild blue yonder.

I read Merle what Peter Guralnick had recently written about him: "He's achieved more success than he ever intended and cannot come to terms with this success."

"That's true," Haggard said softly. "Success has its benefits and its holdbacks. There are just as many in either direction, you know. It's no secret I've been in prison, and I sometimes feel that all I've done since is just secured myself in a prison I can't escape from. Everything is always committed so far ahead. Yet, you wake up one day, and you don't want to do what you're committed to do that day. Or that month. But you got to do it."

"Ever thought of giving it all up and going for freedom?"

Haggard smiled. "I did that. A couple of years ago, I went and got divorced and got married again." Bonnie leaned forward a little to hear better. "And I stopped the schedule until I decided what I wanted to do with the rest of my life. Six months went by. I was free, and all the holdbacks and problems stayed with me. And all the fun was gone. I wasn't performing. But I was still a personality that people recognized and imposed on; I never found that place I could go to and not be recognized. So I came back. And here I am, sitting in a bus in the middle of New York.

"I just kind of knocked on the door of the prison," Haggard said, "and asked to be let back in. And over the past year, I've come to accept it, give up to it, and have fun when I can. Like, when we're working, we can't play everything we want to do. We have hard-core country fans in the audience and that cuts down on the jazz we can play some places. And sometimes you have to get loud and do the old country-boy nightclub act. But somehow or another, we get in enough to please ourselves. I guess I'll stay in this prison. Where else would I go? To a foreign country and act like a man in exile?"

•   •   •

"When I was sixteen," Merle once told country-music chronicler Lois Lazarus, "I was picked up for a robbery I never committed. A rich kid would get a lawyer, an Okie with a record goes to jail."

In many of his songs, Merle writes about folks who have no connections that can do them any good: poor and working-class whites, migrant workers, diverse outcasts. And so too in the novel he's been at, off and on, for some time. He started writing fiction in school when he was about ten, and his grades suffered because he wasn't paying any mind to what he was supposed to be learning.

"That's what's wrong with our school system," Haggard says. "They were boring me with whatever they had to present. I couldn't get out of the classroom yet, so I just wrote. I remember an old report card my mother had: 'Sits staring out the window, scribbling.'"

Now, this novel, says Merle, is "a kind of comedy-murder mystery. Imagine John-Boy in the Waltons being an asshole, putting mirrors on his shoes in school, and still being in the fourth grade when he was sixteen years old. Only reason he kept going to school was to fuck with the girls." (The ones in the higher grades.)

"He finally winds up being arrested for rape. They think he raped and killed this girl, but they find out it wasn't him. It was the old, nasty boy at school," Haggard grins, "the rich man's son. And they proved it by the new model-A tracks at the scene of the crime. This takes place in the Depression."

Haggard is fond of imagining the Depression years. "I could find many reasons for wanting to live back there," he's told Peter Guralnick. "Such as trains was the main method of travel, the glamour of trains always appealed to me. . . . Then again, the music was young. So many things were being done in music, it was wide open back then, electronics had not yet been involved, and basically it was *real*."

But the realness of those open acoustic sounds—when it came to country musicians in the thirties and into the forties—was distorted on recordings. Or so Merle fiercely believes.

"They made those artists sound less than they were," he says, "because the people doing the recording didn't care about this music. They didn't take time to get the full sound quality of artists like Ernest Tubb and Kitty Wells. They made the twang of country singers, for example, sound a lot more pronounced than it actually was. And a lot of other sound parts were missing. Take Bob Wills. They just farted him off. He'd come to Chicago or New York to record, and they didn't know who he was. Just a hick from Oklahoma, and they treated him that way. He was great enough so that he cut on through anyway, and so did some of the others. But the recording people sure did slight the country performers."

"Hey, Roy," Haggard looked toward Nichols who was still grappling with one of the wonders of the electronic age. "Remember the first time you ever heard Lefty Frizzell in a live appearance? He sounded four times better than he did on records, and he *was* four times better."

"Much better," Roy said reflectively. "*Much* better."

By now, country music means a lot more in profits to the record companies, and so there is no electronic slighting of current practitioners. But Haggard is not happy about much that is currently being packaged as "country." He will name no names but is manifestly disgusted by most of what's on the charts.

"There's no free will to their music," he says. "They're very strict, they're very formal, they're very pop. Yet they're being disguised and called country artists, but they don't have it. They got no heart."

"No soul," said Bonnie.

"No soul," Merle echoed.

Haggard's first huge hit, "Okie from Muskogee," started as a joke. As the band bus rolled through East Oklahoma, there was a sign with that town's name, and one of the musicians said, "I bet they don't smoke marijuana in Muskogee." The rest of the band, breaking up from time to time, fell in with more lyrics, and later Merle finished it off. He was astonished and somewhat appalled when it became the anthem of the hardhats. ("We don't burn our draft cards down on Main Street/We like livin' right and being free.") On the other hand, he still resents those who put "Okie" down for, as one critic said, its "beer-belly mentality."

According to Merle, there were at least eighteen meanings to that song when he finally got through with it, and some of them had to do with his family's roots in Muskogee. "My father came from the area," Haggard has said, "worked hard on his farm, was proud of it, and got called white trash once he took to the road as an Okie. And there were a lot of other Okies from around there, proud people whose farms and homes were foreclosed by eastern bankers. And then got treated like dirt. Listen to that line: 'I'm proud to be an Okie from Muskogee.' Nobody had ever said that before in a song."

That night at the Lone Star, Merle Haggard and the Strangers—looking like the James Younger gang with their black suits, Stetsons, and string ties—lit up "Okie" again to piercing yells from the crowd. Watching the composer, what came to my mind, like a split-screen obbligato, was the broken, desperately needful singing of "God Bless America" at the end of *The Deer Hunter.* There were yo-yos who thought that movie, too, had a beer-belly mentality.

One of Merle's numbers has a guy saying: "Someone told my story in a song. He told it all and never missed a line. He even knew I almost lost my mind."

How do you want to be remembered, Merle? "A writer, I guess," he said to Paul Hemphill. "Somebody who did some living and wrote songs about what he knew. Just like Jimmie Rodgers did."

BOB WILLS:
THE TIMELESS FIDDLER

Years ago I worked for a radio station that was aggressively multicultural, long before the term had become so fashionably divisive. Not being affiliated with a network, WMEX had to reach out to the fractious mosaic that was and is Boston. So we had regular programs of Irish, Jewish, Italian, Swedish, Polish, black gospel, and country music.

At the time, being a jazz elitist, all I knew about country bands and singers was that they must be square. I didn't really try to listen to the music until on one country music show I was listlessly hosting I heard a swinging combo—a hot trumpet, a guitarist who sounded as if he'd listened to the first modern jazz guitarist, Charlie Christian, and a fiddler who could have sat in with aplomb at a New York jazz club. And, for punctuation, there were the most extraordinary exhalations of deep pleasure—"Ah haaaaaa!"—underscoring the high spirits of the music.

The band was Bob Wills and His Texas Playboys. The fiddler was Wills, and he was also responsible for that infectious cry every time he heard something going on that he especially liked.

To this day, listening to good music of any kind, I break into a Wills-like "Ah haaaaaa!" It's a high sound, a sort of folk cry if you believe with Louis Armstrong that we are all folk and therefore part of folk music.

Wills came out of Limestone, Texas, born into a family of fiddlers with an enormous repertory of frontier breakdowns and waltzes and other kinetic forms that attracted people to local dances. But young Jim Rob, as he was first called when he came into the world, was particularly obsessed with the blues.

As a child, he played with black kids; he worked alongside blacks in his father's cotton fields in west Texas, and he absorbed their music. His biographer, Charles Townsend, writes that "one of his favorite artists was the Empress of the Blues, Bessie Smith, and while he was still in his teens, he rode nearly fifty miles on horseback to see her in person."

Wills always thought of his music as being primarily for dancers, and if a band knew how to swing, he said, it would make more people want to dance. In Texas and Oklahoma, Wills, very early in his career, drew enthusiastic crowds. When he became a radio star—as Bob Wills and His Light Crust Doughboys—he filled dance halls all over those states.

Novelist J. R. Goddard described the dancers at a typical date in Oklahoma: "Some were hard-shell Baptists, oil workers, and mule farmers. Most of Bob Wills's fans were poor working class . . . just beginning to get electricity in their homes."

Bob Wills and His Texas Playboys, as they were now called, became nationally popular in 1940 with his "New San Antonio Rose" ("Deep within my heart lies a melody, a song of San Antone"). And after the war, Wills broke records just about everywhere he went.

Although eager to keep attracting all these new listeners and dancers with his "western swing," as he preferred to call his music, Wills never diluted the blues and jazz elements of his music. Smokey Dacus, his first drummer, noted that "Bob Wills would not allow music to be put into a straitjacket." Wills liked the freedom of jazz and blues, and his musicians enjoyed improvising as much as he did.

Wills influenced a lot of country players who liked to take risks in their music. One was Merle Haggard, who told me he so admired Wills that he taught himself the violin so he could play Wills's parts from the vintage Texas Playboys songs.

Even after a heart attack and a stroke, Wills kept hoping he would perform again. Charles Townsend, in *The Stars of Country Music* (Avon), tells of Wills having been invited in 1973 to sit on the stand during a Saturday-night dance in Texas: "Determined to play himself, Bob held the fiddle with his left hand and had the bandleader bow it. Not satisfied, Bob took the microphone with his good hand and sang part of an old Bessie Smith song, 'Downhearted Blues.' "

Wills died in 1975. He was seventy years old. Haggard said that to call the music of Bob Wills country music was as narrowly misleading as to say that Louis Armstrong was a trumpet player, period.

Of the Wills reissues—and more keep coming—a particularly illuminating collection is the two-volume CD *Bob Wills and His Texas Playboys Anthology, 1935–1973* (Rhino Records/Sony Music Entertainment, Inc.).

Wills's music has not dated. The combination of jazz, blues, bar stories, and hot strings reaches so freely and resonantly into what Wills called "human feeling" that it retains its immediacy— at its utterly relaxing, flowing best. Ray DeGeer, a former Wills sideman who later played with Gene Krupa and Charlie Barnet, said that Wills "had an uncanny sense of time and tempo." And both, like Count Basie's, turned out to be timeless.

The songs in the anthology include "New San Antonio Rose," "Miss Molly," "Basin Street Blues," "Deep Water," Bennie Moten's "South," and Wills's "Take Me Back to Tulsa," which has a line out of his observant boyhood: "Darkies raise the cotton/White man gets the money."

AT HOME IN HONKY-TONKS

Charlie Parker used to hang out in Charlie's Tavern, a musicians' bar in midtown New York. To the dismay of his acolytes, he liked to play country records on the jukebox. There was reluctance to question the taste of the mighty Bird, but finally a brave jazzman asked him, "How can you stand that stuff?"

Bird looked at him and said, "The stories, man. Listen to the stories!"

Through the years I've found quite a large number of other country-music aficionados with no roots at all in the ways of life in those parts of the country that the music embodies. Some play their George Jones and Lefty Frizzell records behind closed doors for fear of seeming square and sentimental. Others disdain such concealment. For instance, the late Nathan Perlmutter, who was national director of the Anti-Defamation League, of B'nai Brith, was an unabashed collector of Merle Haggard sides.

For both the city fans and those who live where there's never a traffic jam, recent years have been a discouraging time. The sounds that used to be as pure as country water have become thick with violins and trickster electronics. "Crossover" fever has infected many of the established stars and most of the new contenders. As the Statler Brothers keened, "Nobody wants to be country, everybody wants to go pop." Indeed, rhinestone cowboys born in New Jersey came to claim the mantle of Hank Williams.

There has come to be so much pop in country, however, that when a new wave of back-to-the-basics singers made their move, they sounded so fresh and different that they began to sell a lot of records. Among them was Randy Travis, whose first album, *Storms of Life* (Warner Bros. Records), went gold (the industry term for sales of more than half a million sets). And then he won the annual Country Music Association's Horizon (new star) Award. He has since won many other awards and is no longer just a new star.

Travis was brought up on a farm outside Marshville, North Carolina. His father ran a construction company, raised turkeys, and couldn't get enough of country music. His wife felt the same way. Their children, therefore, heard nothing but real country sounds.

By the time Randy Travis was ten, he and his brother were playing at fiddlers' conventions, private parties, VFW halls, and square dances. At fourteen, with his parents watching over him, Mr. Travis began working honky-tonks, which can be described euphemistically as highly informal rooms where you come as you bristlingly are. Or, as Mr. Travis describes the milieu, "There was a fight just about every night."

A singer who can hold the attention of the drinkers and talkers in a honky-tonk has learned how to make his presence felt anywhere. Mr. Travis worked in a Charlotte, North Carolina, club for six years and then went on to Nashville, where he was a combination cook, dishwasher, and singer in a club. One night, as in the dreams of country boys, a Warner Bros. Records executive heard him. Travis put down the skillet.

On *Storms of Life*, Mr. Travis at first sounds like a young Merle Haggard ("I'm a born loner and nothing can get to me for long"). Almost immediately, as with Mr. Haggard, there is also the vulnerability not very far underneath the surface grit. As the album moves on, however, it's clear that Mr. Travis has a style of his own that comes out of thirteen years of learning how to tell stories that are so softly compelling they could gentle down the boisterous honky-tonk clientele.

He sings conversationally. There is no straining for dramatic effect. The people in the stories tell of what's going on inside them, and Mr. Travis becomes each of them so convincingly that their natural presence and cadences create natural drama.

Most of the songs, some of them by Mr. Travis, are what jazz singer Jimmy Rushing used to call he/she songs. In one, a single line touches the essence of a broken marriage: "The saddest thing I've ever seen is my closet all cleaned out."

"Send My Body" has mordant fun with a theme older than twentieth-century country music—the cowboy about to be hanged for a crime he didn't commit but somehow not surprised that's where he wound up. ("Send my body home on a freight train and don't worry none that I don't go first-class. Send my body home on a freight train so everyone can see me when I pass.") Behind Mr. Travis is a swaggering, swinging country-jazz combo in the tradition of Bob Wills and Merle Haggard.

The most quietly powerful song is Mr. Travis's own "Reasons I Cheat." It is told by a balding, middle-aged man in a dead-end job with a wife who talks at him but doesn't see him. However, a "willing young woman" does see him and "has chosen to lay sound asleep by my side." Having this "lady that knows me" is reason enough to cheat, this weary pilgrim observes convincingly.

I asked Randy Travis how, at his age, he was able both to write and sound like this aging lover. "I played a lot of those clubs," he said, "and I talked to so many people in those clubs. I heard a lot of stories."

The last song on the album, "There'll Always Be a Honky Tonk Somewhere," predicts that "there may be factories on the moon and farming in space, but so long as there's a broken heart, there'll be a place to go where good old boys meet good old girls, and the wine and the music flow."

I sure hope so.

After all, many of the legends of country music learned their bardic craft in honky-tonks. These "fightin' and dancin'" clubs, as a survivor described them, were usually on the outskirts of town, where the police were less likely to make regular rounds. Most had dance floors, and in some, a wire screen more or less protected the band from various objects and bodies that might be thrown among the patrons in the course of the night.

To attract and hold the attention of the revelers, a performer had to tell stories with which the crowd could identify. Sheer volume wouldn't do the trick; the drinkers could get a lot louder than the band. It was out of this finishing school—notably in Texas, but in other states as well—that such masters of real-life narratives as Lefty Frizzell, Ernest Tubb, and George Jones emerged. Their natural presence carried them through without loudspeakers that reached the next county.

But the noise in the Texas honky-tonks sounds pastoral by contrast with the huge and hugely distorting amplification systems that now transmogrify even the back-to-basics New Traditionalists when they work auditoriums and some clubs.

In New York's Madison Square Garden, the finale of the 1988 Spring Marlboro Country Music Tour consisted of four superstar acts: Randy Travis, George Strait, the Judds, and Alabama. The first three are, with variations, New Traditionalists. On the other hand, whatever country elements were present in the early days of Alabama have now been electrocuted. No matter how many country awards it keeps winning, Alabama has become a fungible rock group. The Judds are somewhat more credible musically, but not much.

By contrast, Randy Travis has, in three years, won nearly all the awards there are while refusing to cross over to pop. On records and on a car radio, Travis sounds as if he's talking to you late at night in a bar. Yet, in Madison Square Garden, the assaultive sound system takes over his music, crushes the lyrics, and makes him sound like static.

Relentlessly, the rock fan's definition of proper sound level has become standard in auditoriums and many clubs, no matter who plays there. Like some other survivals of the corybantic sixties, this addiction to filling oneself with sound to the very limit of endurance is abusive to the body, mind, and spirit. And it destroys good and bad music alike. As my wife, a devoted country music fan, said as she fled the omnivorous sound machines, "It's like being addicted to the sound of jackhammers and subway trains."

A few weeks before, we had gone to the Lone Star, a club in Greenwich Village that specializes in country music but also has increasingly booked rock groups. Six years before, I saw Merle

Haggard and the Lonesome Strangers there. There was a large, fervent audience, but I could hear every word.

Around the same time, there was an astonishing evening at the Lone Star with Delbert McClinton, the Texas honky-tonker rightly billed as "The King of the White Texas Bluesmen." The crowd, including me, was jammed tight and roaring, but there was no sound distortion as McClinton gloriously sang the blues, without pause, for more than an hour.

But on our later trip to hear McClinton at the Lone Star, we left after fifteen minutes. The club's amplifying system had by now been taken over by the insatiable dybbuk of rock. McClinton's mouth was open, but the words were inaudible.

During the Marlboro Country Music show at the Garden, George Strait, a Texan who always wears a white hat so you'll know he's not a bad guy, presented his straight-ahead, country-swing repertory, which has sold millions of records. An actual cowboy who ran a cattle ranch before hitting the charts, Strait is sort of the Al Gore of country music—easy in manner, self-confident without being arrogant. His music also is likable, but it does not stay in the mind. Lefty Frizzell and Bob Wills need not make room for Strait in the pantheon of country music.

The amplifying system was no more accommodating to New Traditionalist Strait than to Travis, with the result, for example, that when Strait sang a ballad, "You're Something Special to Me," it sounded as if he were addressing the Joint Chiefs of Staff in a high school gym.

Alabama's performance was not harmed by the sound system because its very lifeblood is white noise.

Marlboro donated part of the proceeds from its country-music tour to various projects serving the nation's hungry. The tobacco company also might consider giving a few bucks for hearing aids and lung cancer.

HOT COUNTRY SWING
FROM TEXAS

He was white, but he was playing the blues—on the harmonica—
by the time he was three years old. Herb Ellis later became a
world-class, world-renowned jazz guitarist, always with the blues
in mind. He'd been born on the levee in Farmersville, a place in
northern Texas that Ellis recalls as so bleak that "anybody would
get the blues growing up there."

Like many kids, he could escape from home by putting on the
radio. One of his favorite bands was Bob Wills and His Light
Crust Doughboys, a western swing outfit that was popular in
Texas during the 1930s. Fiddler Bob Wills was in that group for a
time and went on to form the most influential western-swing
band, the jubilant Texas Playboys.

Herb Ellis, meanwhile, was also listening to Charlie Christian,
who invented modern jazz guitar, and he felt the irresistible call
to become a full-time jazzman. He first became widely known as
part of the Oscar Peterson trio in the 1950s. Peterson played a lot
of notes, but underneath that prodigious technique, as Miles
Davis once told me, "He didn't know how to swing."

But Herb Ellis did, and I'd go to hear the Peterson trio because of the depth and blues-driven swing of the guitarist. There was also the joy and energy with which Ellis improvised, and unlike Peterson, he let his solos breathe.

After leaving Oscar Peterson, Ellis did a lot of studio work (the Steve Allen and Merv Griffin shows) and also played clubs and jazz concerts. When he's off the road, he and his wife now live in the Arkansas Ozarks in a retirement community. Ellis is seventy-two, but he can only take so much golf and tennis. He still spends many nights elsewhere taking pleasure in improvising.

I can't think of a jazzman over seventy capable of still getting on a stage who has actually retired.

Musicians need not only to play but also to hear their listeners. It's very difficult to not move, and indeed shout somewhat, when Ellis is playing. "I want my listeners right in there with me," he says.

Over a period of eighteen years, Ellis made thirty albums for the California label Concord—all of them swinging, straightaway jazz. But he has been lured back home to a Texas label, Justice. Its founder, Randall Hage Jamail, came up with an idea that no musician who listened as a boy to the Light Crust Doughboys could reject.

Ellis first made a jazz set for Jamail, but what especially intrigued him was the idea of making a western-swing session. "I wanted," Jamail told the *Houston Post*, "to release something that was fresh and startling because that was my commitment when I signed Herb—to put him in fresh and unique situations."

There always was a tangy Texas sound in Ellis's jazz—an extra thrust, as in tenor saxophonists from Texas—along with traces of country voicings. So it had been with the western swing of Bob Wills's Texas Playboys. Jamail put together a session with Ellis and three former Texas Playboys—the ceaselessly surprising fiddler Johnny Gimble, drummer Tommy Perkins, and pedal steel guitarist Herb Remington. Of Remington, a musician on the date said, "He puts a good floor that you can walk on."

Also on hand was Willie Nelson on acoustic guitar, violinist Bobby Bruce, bassist Tommy Alsup, and pianist Floyd Domino. It is a joyous set. "The excitement level of the recording," Jamail recalls, "was almost childlike. Everybody was having such a good time. And Herb Ellis, too, came to the session almost like a kid."

Most of the songs were recorded in only one or two takes—always a sign that the musicians on a date are really listening to one another. The tunes in *Texas Swings* have a very wide range—from Charlie Parker's "Billie's Bounce" (mislabeled as "Scrapple from the Apple") to "Blues in G," "It Had to Be You," a swinging "The Old Rugged Cross" (not in the standard jazz repertory), and an "America the Beautiful" that can be danced to.

All the players did Bob Wills proud. As Johnny Gimble told John Burnett of National Public Radio, "You could just name any song, and it would come out swinging."

Of Gimble, Burnett noted: "Now sixty-seven, Gimble perfected his phrasing during his years with Bob Wills. He hits the strings two at a time, a technique called double stops, in a way that mimics the riffs of a horn section."

On this set, Ellis, in a way, is a boy again, living out his fantasies as a child listening to the Light Crust Doughboys on the radio. Now he's *in* that music. He's been in jazz for nearly half a century, but on this date, he was born again.

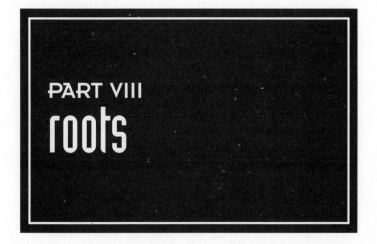

PART VIII
roots

"THERE'LL BE NO DYING OVER THERE"

Some years ago, when I was on the road with Lester Flatt and Earl Scruggs's country-music combo, my place on the bus was as a reporter and a fan of their music, particularly Scruggs's three-finger banjo style. Late one afternoon, while it was still light, the players performed at an open-air gathering in a small mill town in Alabama.

It seemed as if nearly every white person in town—the workers and their families—had come to hear the music. There wasn't much shouting or loud clapping, but just about everyone, including the kids, listened and watched with rapt attention.

When the music stopped and we got back on the bus, I felt sad for those so polite and so intense folks who had obviously wanted more. Sitting next to the dobro player, I said, "Your music means a lot to them."

"Sure," he said. "We come from places like that. We know who they are, and they know that."

Since then, much of country music has become so deracinated that someone from New Jersey or with a degree from Smith

College can go to Nashville and wind up a country star. But there are still some stubborn defenders of the unalloyed traditions of mountain music, bluegrass, and the kind of honky-tonk sounds and stories embodied in Hank Williams songs. Those are the country songs you won't hear on elevators.

To serious country musicians—and their music is as serious as jazz or Beethoven—a continuing teacher and legend is Ralph Stanley, a subtly resourceful banjo picker whose singing has been described by Bill Malone—the premier historian of these forms—as "one of the most unmistakably rural voices in country music . . . a haunting, almost sepulchral voice." At sixty-seven, Stanley has been on the music bus for some forty-seven years, most of them as leader of the Clinch Mountain Boys. His coleader until he died in 1966 was his brother, Carter, an equally penetrating musician. As the Stanley Brothers, they made recordings that are as treasured by country aficionados as rare takes of Charlie Parker are outside the mountains.

The Stanley brothers were born and grew up in the hill country of southwestern Virginia. Their father, a sawmill operator, liked to sing such brooding old songs as "A Man of Constant Sorrow." Their mother, a true musician, was a vigorous practitioner of the two-finger "clawhammer" way of stirring up the banjo. And the family attended the Old Regular Baptist Church, where the singing was rugged and individual.

The story of the Stanleys and the mountain traditions that shaped them—as well as absorbing interviews with musicians who have played with Ralph Stanley—are in a carefully researched book, *Traveling the Highway Home: Ralph Stanley and the Traditional World of Bluegrass Music* (University of Illinois Press). The author is John Wright, a professor of Latin and literature at Northwestern University. More to the point, he's a columnist for the *Banjo Newsletter*.

There is also a remarkable oral Festshrift in honor of Ralph Stanley. In two CDs—all in one package, along with the lyrics to the songs—there is the musical odyssey of Ralph Stanley and of what he describes as "the old-time style of what they call bluegrass music." He means his own classical approach. In *Saturday Night and Sunday Morning*, Stanley is joined on various tracks by a pride of singers who pay him tribute by the integrity of their own music.

Among them are Emmylou Harris, Dwight Yoakam, Charlie Waller, Ricky Scaggs, Charlie Sizemore, Bill Monroe (the seemingly eternal father of bluegrass), George Jones, and Tom T. Hall. Some are alumni of the Clinch Mountain Boys, and all try successfully to blend into the collective spirit of old-time mountain music.

In the secular *Saturday Night* set, there are such grim echoes of old English ballads as "Banks of the Ohio," the confession of a rejected lover who drowned the young woman and "watched her as she floated down." The other love songs seldom end in satisfaction, but that's why the term "high, lonesome harmonies" is often used in characterizing this music.

The second CD, *Sunday Morning,* includes gloriously moving, down-home religious music. There are also tales of loss that can't be made whole even in church. And, of course, there are danger signs pointing to ever-present temptation. Charlie Sizemore, in "The Old Crossroad," sings:

Oh my brother take this warning
Don't let old Satan hold your hand.
You'll be lost in sin forever
You'll never reach the promised land. . . .
The old crossroad now is waiting
Which one are you goin' to take?

In "Heaven's Bright Shore," arranged and with new verses by Ralph Stanley, he sings with a new pilgrim learning the tradition, twenty-one-year-old Alison Kraus. The song is a vision that sometimes can soften hard times in the mountains:

On heaven's bright shore
There'll be no dying over there
Not one little grave, not one little grave . . .
And no one up there will say goodbye.

On all the tracks there is the authority of performers who are among that rare group of people who enjoy what they do to make a living. The Ralph Stanley set is available from the Freeland Recording Co., Route 12, Asbury, WV 24916.

There are a good many country-music stations around the nation, but not many are likely to play any selections from this album. It's too classical. But Ralph Stanley still has audiences. He appears from time to time on such television shows as "Austin City Limits" and at festivals. Also, as John Wright notes in his book on Ralph Stanley, he keeps playing for the kind of people I saw, with Flatt and Scruggs, in that Alabama mill town—at "tiny schoolhouse auditoriums accessible only by twisted mountain roads that offer a continual challenge to the band bus." That, says Young, is "Ralph Stanley Country."

"THERE'S FIRE ON THE MOUNTAIN AND THERE'S FIRE IN THE FIDDLE"

Charleston, West Virginia—In the spring of every year, fiddlers, singers, banjo pickers, and virtuosi of the lap dulcimer, among other instruments, celebrate the music of West Virginia at the state's Cultural Center on the state capitol grounds here. It's called the Vandalia Gathering, and participants come from the "hollers" (the hollows hidden in the steep mountains), from Deadfall Mountain, and from most every county.

The families, like the music, go way back. One of fiddler Ernie Carpenter's forebears, for instance, was born under a rock overhang during an Indian raid in the eighteenth century. Older than that ancestor is the tune "Billy in the Low Ground," performed by fiddler Delbert Hughes. The farewell to Billy goes back to the reign of William and Mary.

In another song, the Morris Brothers toast their colleagues: "There's fire on the Mountain and there's fire in the fiddle . . . They learn their tunes from each other, so the music never dies."

The West Virginia Department of Culture and History, which hosts the annual Vandalia Gathering, took a line out of the Morris

Brothers' song for the title of its lively two-LP set, *The Music Never Dies: A Vandalia Sampler, 1977–1987*. Folklorists can find multiple layers of cross-cultural connections over centuries in the music, but you don't have to be a specialist to be drawn into the dream-like, high, lonesome sound of "Elkhorn Ridge" as sung and played by Ron Mullenn, who learned it from his mother on the family sheep farm. And there's a wide range of bravura fiddling for high-stepping dancing. Among the sizzling banjoists is Phoeba Paroons, who learned to pick from her father many years ago. As she says on the recording: "My music that I play is old-time from way back. I never learned no new tunes, and I ain't fig-uring on it."

Many of the players, however, want to pass on not only the vintage tunes but also the spirit of the music that can move new generations to create songs in the tradition. One of the founders of the Vandalia Gathering, David Morris, a practitioner of the Autoharp, told *Southern Living* magazine: "I used to look over my shoulder and worry that the music wouldn't continue. But it will. It's the language of our mountains. As surely as we learn to talk, we learn this too."

But it takes some doing to successfully expose youngsters to these indigenous sounds. After all, their forebears didn't have radios and the other distracting sounds of the outside world dur-ing the centuries the Vandalia tradition was being shaped. Connecting West Virginia's young to their heritage is a priority of Norman Fagan, the state's commissioner of the Culture and History Department. "One thing we do," he told me, "is bring young people into the annual gathering. They're able to listen to, talk, and learn from the old-timers.

"It's all very informal. Also, through our heritage programs, we bring West Virginia musicians into the schools. Teachers can apply for grants to bring the performers into the classroom . . . Furthermore, appearances by musicians, the kind who are heard at Vandalia, can be arranged by us for any college, university, or community group."

The Department of Culture and History produced *The Music Never Dies* on its Elderberry label. It's available through the Cultural Center Shop, the Cultural Center, State Capitol Complex, Charleston, WV 25305. Another distinctive recording in the shop—though not produced by the state—is *U.S. Senator Robert Byrd/Mountain Fiddler.*

On the floor of the Senate and in his many television appearances, Byrd is invariably formal, meticulously conscious of his position and privileges, and without—as blues singers might say—much "soul." The senator as musician, however, is a Byrd of quite different plumage. He plays hot, foot-tapping fiddle, and on the recording he credits his initial passion for country music to his wife's father, a coal miner who played the violin.

But it is the singing Byrd who provides the most tender surprise. The senator becomes gently, hauntingly compelling in "Come Sundown She'll Be Gone." Waking, barely hearing the front door closing, Byrd remembers: "the soft touch of her lips, Lord, was like a whisper on my cheek . . . the soft sheets still feel warm where she laid upon my bed."

How many other United States senators can sing of love—not votes—with such credibility?

In *The Vandalia Sampler* the Morris Brothers sing: "They say the fiddle is a riding horse, and the devil is in the night, but I believe the fiddlers are touched by God's own clear blue light."

It could be that in the music of West Virginia there's something of both as the fire burns on the mountain, in the fiddle, and in the blood.

A RIDE ON THE GOSPEL TRAIN

They used to come into the radio station where I worked every Friday night. Generations of black men, soft-spoken, conservatively dressed, grouped in quartets, waiting their turn to participate in the black gospel hour. I would watch through the studio window as these singers created tidal waves of rhythms and soaring harmonies that my composition teacher had never imagined.

I found out that all these conductors on the gospel train had day jobs. On Sundays, they performed at various churches, singing such reminders as "(You Can't Hurry God) He's Right on Time" and "Move on Up a Little Higher."

In the early 1950s, walking in Harlem, I was suddenly enveloped in musical explosions of exultation. I looked up and walked up to the second floor of Daddy Grace's building to see a gospel choir driven by tambourines and trombones. It was swinging at least as hard as the Count Basie band. The only other such total immersion in music I've experienced was among the dancing, singing, almost levitating Hasidim of Brooklyn.

From jazz musicians I found out that as children most of them had been bathed in gospel music, usually in Holiness churches. They were grateful for those roots, in part because white jazz musicians didn't have them. In the midfifties, when Dave

Brubeck and white-bread "West Coast jazz" were becoming exceptionally popular, black musicians in New York found an effective way to retaliate. I went to a rehearsal of a new combo co-led by drummer Art Blakey and pianist Horace Silver, and the musicians were burnishing a piece called "The Preacher." It had the infectiously rocking rhythms and the soul-driven "cry" of the gospel quartets I used to hear at the radio station.

"Now, that's something the white boys can't play," Blakey said with satisfaction. "Not with any authority." The group became the successful Jazz Messengers, and elsewhere black musicians—Cannonball Adderley, Milt Jackson, Charles Mingus—also put gospel music into the forefront of jazz.

Meanwhile, as the years go on, black men of various ages and occupations continue to appear in quartets in black churches on Sundays. And some singing gospel groups are also playing night-clubs on occasion. That kind of crossover used to be a cardinal sin. Music aimed at God could not be directed at drunkards and adulterers. But now, for instance, the vintage Gospel Hummingbirds of Oakland, California, work blues clubs and rock concerts. They feel it's a common language, after all.

Also, recording companies are releasing a revealing range of historic gospel performances. Rhino Records has issued three volumes of *Jubilation!: Great Gospel Performances* on CD. The artists on these songs, recorded from 1929 through 1980, are both white and black. As in blues, country music, and jazz, much borrowing and transmuting went on between the races.

The first two *Jubilation!* sets are of black gospel, including Mahalia Jackson, who had been a domestic and a nurse until Decca talent scouts heard her sing at a funeral. Also present on Volume 1 are the Famous Blue Jay Singers of Birmingham, Alabama, the Swan Silvertones, and Aretha Franklin. Also the Dixie Hummingbirds with "Christian's Automobile." ("I'm not worrying about my parking space/I just want to see the Savior face to face.")

Considering the abundance of compelling but hardly famous gospel quartets I used to hear in Boston, before I came to New York, I expect there were, and still are, many others around the country unknown except in local churches or to aficionados. Volume 2 of *Jubilation!*, for example, has the Original Gospel

Harmonettes from Birmingham, Alabama, and the Norfolk Jubilee Quartet. Much better known, because they have appeared in secular settings, are The Staple Singers, whose "Uncloudy Day" conjures up mysterious danger in the gathering twilight.

The third volume is white country gospel, starting with Hank Williams's unwittingly ironic "I Saw the Light" (he never did) and moving to Patsy Cline's "Life's Railway to Heaven." Cline was as naturally sensuous in religious as in two-timing music. Also indispensable to this kind of collection are "The Great Speckled Bird" (not Charlie Parker), sung by Roy Acuff, and "Will the Circle Be Unbroken," with a number of country luminaries. ("Undertaker, please drive slow/This body, I hate to see her go.")

Country music like this used to appeal to Charlie Parker, and in this last Rhino volume, there is a performance by Webb Pierce of "Bugle Call from Heaven" that both distills the message of black and white gospel music and might also have appealed to Bird's continual self-questioning, which was not unlike that of certain wayward white country stars such as George Jones: "When that bugle sounds in heaven/Can you stand that last inspection?/Can you answer that final bugle call?"

One of the most penetrating, satisfying gospel singers was Sam Cooke of the Soul Stirrers. He later became one of the great crowd-lifters in after-dark secular soul music. Cooke was killed by a motel manager who claimed he attacked her. I remember gospel singers telling me that's the kind of thing that happens when you cross over. And then what will you say when that final bugle call sounds?

Gospel music, they pointed out, is serious music, as serious as life itself.

THE LEGEND WHO REFUSED TO
BECOME JUST A MEMORY

The slender, long-haired, fiercely shy singer was unknown when she took the stage at the 1959 Newport Folk Festival; but the penetrating force of her "achingly pure soprano," as one critic put it, made her an overnight star who was soon to become a legend.

A year later I brought Joan Baez to Robert Herridge, the most original and literate television producer then or since. Herridge and I had worked together on "The Sound of Jazz" with Billie Holiday, Count Basie, Thelonious Monk, and other nonpareils. He wanted to do a similarly uncompromising folk-music program. I had already recommended Lightnin' Hopkins and Cisco Houston. Herridge was mesmerized by Baez's voice—but not by Baez.

"The bitch is nineteen years old," Herridge complained to me, "and she thinks she's Thomas Mann!" Baez would not do the show unless she was in complete control of what she would sing, the set behind her (or rather there should be no set at all), and a few other things.

The shyness had gone, but the integrity became stronger and stronger. In 1963, when many folksingers were plotting how to get on ABC-TV's popular "Hootenanny," Baez turned down an invitation because the show had blacklisted Pete Seeger.

Meanwhile, she sold more albums than any folksinger had ever sold. At first her repertory consisted mainly of centuries-old English ballads, which she sang so convincingly that onstage she seemed to be of that time. Then there were occasional acutely contemporary songs of protest against the Vietnam War, against bigotry, against complacency. Some were written by the barely known Bob Dylan, whom she introduced to larger audiences by bringing him along on her concert tours.

The Wild Jewish Boy and the Madonna on the Half Shell (as Baez referred to herself) became lovers for a while, an event that gratified the fantasies of many of their fans, for Baez and Dylan were the only royalty these American romantics recognized.

During the 1960s and after, Baez, far more than any other performer in any medium, became part of what she sang about. She marched with Dr. Martin Luther King in Grenada, Mississippi; raised money and gave time to César Chavez's striking farmworkers and Amnesty International; was twice arrested and imprisoned for helping to block an armed-forces induction center in Oakland, California; and became a thoroughly knowledgeable proselytizer for nonviolence. She had absorbed the works of Gandhi and, being Baez, disputed him on a number of points.

Baez went on to found the Humanitas International Human Rights Committee and traveled through much of the world to defy—nonviolently—various repressive agents of authoritarian regimes. She could also make unexpected Scarlet Pimpernel visits at home. Some years ago I was reporting on the vicious anti-Semitic hostilities that were being directed at Susan Shapiro, a high school senior in Randolph, Massachusetts. Shapiro was a Reagan Republican but objected to saluting "a piece of cloth" (the American flag) during mandatory morning devotions in school.

Shapiro became a pariah at the high school, and threats of violence were delivered to her home, usually with such patriotic comments as "Hitler should have finished the job." I called the young woman in that small town one day, and she said, "Hold on, there's someone here who wants to talk to you." It was the Scarlet Pimpernel. Baez had come to give Susan support. A song wouldn't do. She had to be there.

Once in a while Baez would brood about her prospects as a singer. Rock had captured the vast majority of the young. People of her age and older still came to her concerts, but, as she recently told the *New York Times*, "they were bringing their children who were miserable because they didn't want to be there. I felt like rescuing them."

In between her sometimes perilous journeys on behalf of human rights, Baez tried various approaches to making albums that might actually have respectable sales again. Furthermore, her voice had deepened and was no longer "achingly pure." I heard one of her recorded attempts at being with-it, and I hoped she would not let it be released. But she did. It was an all-too-earnest attempt to reach the kids and had little of Baez's character in it—and none of the swift, self-deprecatory wit of her maturing years. The recording went nowhere.

Finally, Baez, by being Baez, came up with the right combination in *Play Me Backwards* (Virgin Records). First of all, it was recorded in Nashville, where the studio players, given half a chance to breathe on their own, are more loose and therefore enlivening than their counterparts anywhere else. Furthermore, the small backup band—a rhythm section with African and Latin tinges, along with the dobro, among other guitars—crisply energizes Baez without tripping her.

The songs—some by Baez and others by Janis Ian, Mary Chapin-Carpenter, John Hiatt, and Ron Davies—have intelligent lyrics that may connect with the lives of some of the listeners. There is a graceful, mordant love song ("Amsterdam"); Baez's emancipation of her twenty-two-year-old son, Gabriel ("I'm with You . . . So It's Time to Set You Free"); a disturbingly graphic "The Dream Song"; and Mary Chapin-Carpenter's "Stone in the Road," a highly distilled account of the passage from pledging allegiance in the classroom to pledging more of oneself in a grownup job.

What makes it all come together, of course, is a Baez who has gotten her confidence back. The voice is strong, and with more warmth than before. Her sense of dynamics, always astute, has not left her; and she is more secure with time, with letting the beat flow, than she ever was.

Baez has not abandoned her other vocation as the Scarlet Pimpernel, but now she can do those necessary works without having to worry as to whether there is still a place for her as a pure songster. And she'll continue to do the unexpected in either field—as when, some years ago, she told her liberal admirers that if they were truly concerned about oppressed people, "that includes policemen, who must be some of the most oppressed people in this society."

PART IX

when the saints
go marching in

DANNY BARKER:
A VERY LONG
LIFE IN JAZZ

I have ten different voices: my intelligent voice, my jazz voice, my night-life voice, my day-life voice, black Northern voice, black Southern voice. All the various voices you have to have when you have a brown or black paint job, you see.

—Danny Barker, from a profile by Michael Tisserand,
Louisiana Endowment for the Humanities,
Summer 1993

I expect that my most long-lasting book will be the one that has no words of mine in it. In 1955, Holt, Rinehart & Winston published *Hear Me Talkin' to Ya*, a history of jazz—as told entirely by the musicians themselves. My co-orchestrator was the late Nat Shapiro, a remarkably amiable and knowledgeable man with a deep love for the music.

A book, like an article, ought to start swinging from note one. And because of the generosity of Danny Barker, a New Orleans jazzman with a memory like a tape recorder, the first chorus of *Hear Me Talkin' to Ya*—his memories of New Orleans—set the groove, the rhythm wave, for the whole book:

> One of my pleasantest memories as a kid growing up in New Orleans was how a bunch of us kids, playing, would suddenly hear sounds. It was like a phenomenon, like the Aurora Borealis. The sounds of men playing would be so clear, but we wouldn't be sure where they were coming from.
>
> So we'd start trotting, start running—"It's this way!" "It's that way!"—And sometimes, after running for a while, you'd find you'd be nowhere near that music. But that music could come on you any time like that. The city was full of the sounds of music . . .

On March 13, Danny Barker died in that city of music. He was eighty-five. Three years ago, he was designated a jazz master by the National Endowment for the Humanities, which also presented this musician of many voices with a lifetime achievement award. He was honored as well by the postal service with a cachet envelope.

Danny took note of all this with pleasure, but he never put on airs, as they used to say. "I'm a jazz musician," he told his friend and chronicler, Michael Tisserand. "I never studied to be no world's greatest. I play music for a living. I'm content to play parties, where people are enjoying themselves."

Tisserand tells of Danny Barker's skeptical reaction when he got a call saying he'd been included in the Jazz Hall of Fame. "You've got all the giants of jazz up there," Barker said. "Why are you putting me up there—seriously. Because I don't play a lot of solos."

Well, Danny was told, "very few people can say they've played with King Oliver, Jelly Roll Morton, Charlie Parker, and Dizzy Gillespie. And they hired you more than once."

Danny also worked with Louis Armstrong, Bunk Johnson, Sidney Bechet, Red Allen, and Dexter Gordon, among scores more.

He was always watching and taking notes. "I'm born under the sign of the goat," Danny Barker used to say. "The goat, he's very observant. He's got great big eyes and he looks straight at you . . . A musician sitting on a stand, he's watching—everybody."

As a kid, he was watching in New Orleans's Storyville: "There are some trumpet players who died that you never hear about. Now, Chris Kelly was a master and played more blues than Louis Armstrong, Bunk Johnson, and anybody you ever knew . . . He was dark of color, low on finance, Baptist from birth . . . Chris could play slow gut-struts until all the dancers were exhausted and dripping wet.

"His masterpiece was 'Careless Love,' preached slow and softly with a plunger. He always played it at twelve o'clock, just before intermission. He'd blow a few bars . . . and his fans would rush about, seeking their loves because that dance meant close embracing, cheek-to-cheek whisperings of love, kissing, and belly-rubbing."

Danny had big ears, as Lester Young might have said. He treated melodies the way he treated his instruments. Or, as Michael Tisserand described Danny's relationship with his guitar in the New Orleans magazine *OffBeat*: "Danny Barker's hand runs down the back of her neck and trails the sharp curves of her body. 'Just like an eighteen-year-old girl,' says Barker, turning his guitar over and polishing its back."

Danny Barker was one of the best rhythm-section guitarists in all of jazz. It was his jazz pulse—through the time zones of various jazz styles—that enabled him to be at home with swingers, boppers, and homeboys.

When Dizzy Gillespie joined Cab Calloway's band, he had to find time and space to hear the music that was inside his head but was not in the band's arrangements. Calloway himself hated the new music. So Dizzy and bassist Milt Hinton would go up on the roof between sets to stretch themselves. Musically sometimes Danny Barker would join them.

"Dizzy would blow his new ideas in chord progressions," Barker recalled, "and he and Hinton would experiment on different ideas and melodic patterns."

Among the mistakes I made during my year as an A&R man for Candid Records years ago was failing to record Danny all by himself. As jazz historian Richard Allen told the New Orleans *Times-Picayune* after Danny's death: "He could play extremely subtly on guitar. In an apartment or a home he could show you some of the soft things. Danny could play those sweet love songs from the '20s and '30s—play those beautiful harmonies that you just don't get in a nightclub atmosphere. It's a shame that was never captured on a recording."

Danny finally returned home in 1965 and for ten years was assistant curator of the New Orleans Jazz Museum. For eight years he was grand marshal of the Onward Brass Band, and of course, he gigged continually around the city.

Danny Barker's passion those years was reaching and teaching the young about their musical roots—through his work with the Fairview Baptist Church Marching Band.

In *Jazztimes* magazine, Wynton Marsalis recalled:

I played in his band when I was eight. He used to get all the young guys. We'd rehearse in this apartment in New Orleans, across the street from the St. Mark's Community Center in the eighth ward.

When I was playing with him, I was totally not serious! I didn't even like to carry my horn for a two-hour parade, marching in the street. I was eight years old and dumb.

Danny used to inspire us to practice, teach us songs, and take time with the whole band ... As I grew older, I began to realize how significant he is, and how great a man he is. When I was a young man, I just didn't know. ...

Danny Barker could always tell you stories about the older musicians. But I didn't realize the value of a man with that type of knowledge ... He's a man who's been dedicated to something for more than sixty years, and was great at it sixty years ago.

Now the richness of his experience and his love for the music comes through his playing. I can't even describe how it feels to be able to recognize how great somebody like him is.

On National Public Radio, Wynton's father, Ellis—a master teacher and resourceful pianist—said of Danny's work with kids to revive the brass-band tradition in New Orleans: "He would just gather up these kids, you know, and start teaching them all of these old songs, like 'Over in the Glory Land,' 'When the Saints Go Marching In,' 'Bye and Bye,' and of course, my sons, both Wynton and Branford, played with him when they were very, very young."

But, Ellis Marsalis continued, "to describe Danny as a teacher is limiting Danny, and at the same time, giving people a different conception of what he really was. As we know teachers to be, Danny was not that.

"Danny was a great inspirer of people. He could make kids want to go out and learn information that he couldn't just give them. He could organize them, he could show them how to do things that pertained to music and also its relationship to life. You can't get that from somebody who just knows techniques and how to manipulate an instrument."

Not, alas, having been a member of the Fairview Baptist Church Brass Band, I didn't know Danny as that kind of inspirer. But I did learn from him whenever we talked. As a survivor—singer Joe Williams's highest praise for those involved in jazz—Danny had seen much of the world, high and low. When he expressed an appraisal of somebody, I trusted his judgment. He wasn't cynical, but he was ever watchful.

Danny enjoyed who he was and how he had come there. And he sure took great pleasure from music, from shaping it to reflect his life. It's a shame he wasn't able to hear the brass-band music at his funeral. Roxane Orgill—who writes for the *Wall Street Journal* about a range of musical scenes with precise originality—was there:

> It was a great, big noisy funeral with a band of 40 musicians or more, six grand marshals and a second line numbering in the many hundreds. . . .
>
> The grand marshals adjusted the sashes across their chests bearing the names of their bands (Olympia, Tuxedo) or clubs (Money Wasters); and the paper doves perched on their shoulders, representing the flight to the hereafter.
>
> At the first drumroll, adults and children appeared from who knows where to dance alongside, forming the so-called "second line." One of the marshals waved a picture of Barker . . . Trumpets, trombones and saxophones

locked in harmonic and melodic step, formed a thick block of sound, from which countermelodies on a clarinet or soprano sax spiraled up like cigarette smoke. "In the Sweet By and By," "Lord, Lord, Lord," "What a Friend We Have in Jesus." Second liners sang along. One could see their open mouths and ecstatic eyes, but their voices were all but lost in the mournful march of bass drums and blasts of tuba.

Thinking of his funeral, I remembered Danny's book, *A Life in Jazz* (Oxford University Press). A plain title and so full and influential a life. Michael Tisserand once asked Danny what he thought is his greatest contribution.

"I'm a jazzman," Danny Barker said, "playing a jazz instrument."

I last saw Danny in New Orleans. He was in his seventies and was planning to write another book. He had boxes and boxes overflowing with memories. There was time to get on with it. But, as used to be chanted at New Orleans funerals years ago, "the butcher cut him down."

LAST CHORUS

In Nashville, when I was coming up, our piano player was a barber. He couldn't play but one or two tunes, but he could play the blues. He knew the blues. They always knew the blues. I don't know where they get it from.

—Doc Cheatham

I never looked behind me to find out what other people were playing or doing. I just keep going, looking for new ideas, practicing. I'm never bored. There's always a new way to play anything.

—Dizzy Gillespie

In the summer of 1993, a three-block area of New York City's East Village—on Avenue B along Tompkins Square Park, between Seventh and Tenth streets—was officially renamed Charlie Parker Place. It is an area of many cultures, some of them dangerous—particularly, of course, 'round midnight and after.

Bird lived, for a time, in a basement apartment in a four-story white stone building that has survived at 151 Avenue B. He used to say of this East Village neighborhood, "I like the people around here. They don't give you no hype."

Charlie Parker was a master of hype—the most accomplished

at that bunco art I have ever seen. But there was no hype in his music.

Gary Giddins wrote in *The Triumph of Charlie Parker* (Beech Tree Books): "As with Mozart, the facts of Charlie Parker's life make little sense because they fail to explain his music. Perhaps his life is what his music overcame. And overcomes."

For many years I spent most of my time in the company of jazz musicians. Since then, much of my writing has been about the law, politics, and the nation's growing obsession with death: euthanasia, physician-assisted suicide, the abortion wars, and the growing lust for capital punishment while Congress and the Supreme Court make it harder and harder for those on death row—predominantly black—to get hearings that might prove their innocence or the unconstitutionality of their trials.

I think that my opposition to officially imposed death—from euthanasia to capital punishment—comes largely from my exposure, from an early age, to the life force that is jazz, and that so characterizes its players in many different ways.

Part of that force is the warmth of the bonds between the musicians, often between generations. As Charles Mingus said, "I always liked those older cats. I always liked to play with them. Nothing ever could keep them down."

And Cecil Taylor, telling the British interviewer Les Tomkins of musicians who inspired him—Duke Ellington, Chick Webb, Fats Waller, Jimmie Lunceford: "They were beacons, lights indicating a certain direction. There was a way they looked, a way that you felt when you heard what they did, that you wanted to become a part of. And you *strove* to become a part of it. It's a question of trying to achieve that image in sound, in thought, in feeling, in being."

There is a growing library of films that illuminate some of the relationships among jazz players off and on the stand—and among generations. The movie that most clearly stays in my mind is *The Last of the Blue Devils,* a ninety-one-minute film made by Bruce Ricker who went to Kansas City some years ago to teach and practice law but got caught in the exhilaration of the music and has never been the same since. He has made more jazz films and also distributes many by other documentary makers through his Rhapsody Films in New York.

For two years Ricker spent his weekends with those survivors of the glory years of Kansas City jazz who had never left or who had come back to ease into eternity with friends who had shared their best times. Then, in March 1974, the filmmaker set up a reunion of hometown swingers and long-gone wanderers in what used to be the black union hall and is now a private enclave, the Mutual Musicians Foundation. Count Basie showed up, as did Joe Turner, among others; and Ricker's cameras picked up their conversations as well as their music.

A year later he arranged for another gathering. Those who had stayed in Kansas City jammed, for the first time in many years, with such visitors from the past as bassist Gene Ramey, guitarist Eddie Durham, and the professor, the calmly authoritative alto saxophonist Buster Smith, who has influenced so many players, not the least of them Charlie Parker. Also present was Jo Jones.

Mr. Jones was as incandescent, graceful, and precise now as he was when I was first granted an audience with him in my teens and he decided I was going to be one of "the kiddies" he would instruct musically and morally. Most of his "kiddies" have been fledgling musicians, but he saved a few slots for the ungifted, and his pastorate was worldwide.

Many of the musicians at the two gatherings that make up the film were once associated with the Oklahoma City Blue Devils, a powerfully rolling unit started by bassist Walter Page in the 1920s. It was the first big band Count Basie had ever been in. Other alumni have included Lester Young, Jo Jones, Jimmy Rushing, and Buster Smith. Page took the name of the band from the intrepid barbed-wire cutters during the range wars between farmers and cattlemen.

The Blue Devils come alive again in the tales exchanged during the movie. So do Charlie Parker, Lester Young, and others of the dead. Startlingly, Lester's voice softly leaps through from an old tape: "The way I play, I try not to be a repeater pencil." None of them were repeater pencils, and they positively glow with their pride in each having had something of his own to add to those long Kansas City nights and days when there were so many clubs and so much pulsing music in the air.

The banter among the improvisers is among the delights of the movie. Playing music that is irreverent by nature, jazzmen are egalitarian kidders. As when Count Basie, by far the most successful member of the old gang—in terms of art as well as income—returns to the old black union hall toward the start of the movie. He is wearing his habitual yachting cap. As Basie comes in the door, one of the players who never left and is known now, on the outside, only to earnest discographers, shouts, "Here comes Basie! Just got off the ship. Big Wheel, you left the ship outside?" Basie grins broadly, for there is no more malice in that greeting than in Joe Turner singing "Hello, little girl, don't you remember me?"

Big Joe Turner, huge Joe Turner, singing in the film with such easeful authority, such economy of phrasing and gesture, that nothing has ever seemed more natural than the blues rising from this long-term watcher of the night. At a table with Jay McShann and other seasoned souls who remember Joe when he was little and tireless, Turner tells of "a big, fine chick in Texas. Slept with a forty-five on the dresser, a pearl-handle nickel-plated, so you don't mess up too much, you hear. If she say, 'Sit down,' you sit down. When she say, 'You have breakfast,' you have breakfast."

Along with the playing and singing, there is some tap dancing—by Speedy Huggins, with swifter turns of surprise than I would have thought possible for a man of his years. Jo Jones, himself a dancer way back, chuckles, sitting beside me. "Do you know that man quit dancing, twenty-five years ago?" Jo does not wait for an answer. "When I came into town for this film, I told Huggins, 'You go home and get your dancing shoes.' Now you see. *That's* what keeps you alive. He never should have stopped. Nobody should stop."

The faces in *The Last of the Blue Devils*! Since I was a kid, those jazz faces have fascinated me. Pee Wee Russell, Billie, Mingus, Duke, Red Allen, Roy Eldridge, Coleman Hawkins, Lester. And later, Monk, Dizzy, Bird, Miles, Coltrane. There is so much American history in those faces. And independence.

Every tub on its own bottom, as Basie once said. And with the independence, so much warmth, though sometimes, as with Lester, you have to look through the shyness. When I was a kid, these faces were not like those of most other adults I knew. And they still aren't. They tell so much more.

So in this movie. Jay McShann, every inch of his broad face so manifestly enjoying the talk and the music. The usually watchful Basie, serenely surrendering to memories of a time when the music never stopped. Indomitable Joe Turner, looking as if the future was anybody else's business but his, thinks of Piney Brown, who owned the Sunset back then and who loved jazz musicians.

> Yes, I dreamed last night
> I was standing on 18th and Vine
> Well, I shook hands with Piney Brown
> Well, I just couldn't keep from crying

Listening, sometimes talking, is a lively man of considerable years with a searching face. He listens carefully and seems to be trying to go past the words to catch some further meaning. He is Ernest Walter Williams, who, Basie testifies, was the Blue Devils' "drummer, manager, conductor, runner, buddy, and everything else that goes with it."

Ernest Williams tells of what the music has meant to him. It consumed him. "My wife said, 'You either give up music or give up me!' I said, 'You got to give me up, and I'll keep the music!'"

As I watch the film, Jo Jones whispers, "He came back to Kansas City from Sacramento, where he was head of the musicians' union. He came back to die. And he came back to talk to the kiddies. He's always talked to the kiddies. He was doing it in Kansas City when I first came there. He'd feed young musicians and tell them how to dress. There was a black tailor downtown who'd take our measurements uptown, and then bring the clothes back up. It was a great city for music, but blacks couldn't buy clothes downtown."

In the movie, briefly, there is Ernest Walter Williams, standing on the corner of Twelfth and Vine and talking to a number of black kids: "Don't use your head as a hat rack. Go to school and get an education, and stop thinking you're smart. I'm your friend, not your enemy. That's Ernest Walter Williams talking. Sixty-nine years old. Can you make it? I made it! Will you?"

> Well, I been to Kansas City
> Oh, everything is really all right
> Yes, I been to Kansas City
> Well, and everything is really all right
> And the boys, they'll jump and swing
> Well, until broad daylight
> 'Cause that's there where the world started
> Everything's going to be all right

Index

Armstrong, Louis (*con't.*)
   Gillespie on "that Armstrong grin," 105
   High Society with Crosby, 60
   as jazz-singer, 51, 52
   on living with his horn, 138
   Red Allen with, 106
   singing instrument, 142
   on Waller's gregarious nature, 121
   Woody Shaw and, 97
Art Blakey's Jazz Messengers, 97, 145, 187
"Ask Me Now," 66
"Austin City Limits" (PBS-TV), 182
"Autumn in New York," 134
"Avenue C," 118

Baez, Joan, 189, 190–92
Baha'i faith, 81–82
Bailey, Buster, 107
Bailey, Dave, 86
Bailey, Mildred, 52
Baker, Dorothy, 108
Baker, Harold "Shorty," 21
Balliett, Whitney, xv–xvi, 89
Banjo Newsletter, 180
Banjo-pickers, 179–80, 184
"Banks of the Ohio," 181
Barker, Danny, 195–200
  on Chris Kelly, 197
  on his ten voices, 195
  on New Orleans music, 196
Barnet, Charlie, 4, 25, 61, 167
Bartók's Second Piano Concerto, 77, 85
Basie, Count, xvi, 19, 25, 35, 41, 90, 129, 137, 150, 167, 186, 189
  All-Stars, 52
  Carnegie Hall tribute, xiii–xiv, 38–39
  definition of jazz, 32, 141–42
  and Fats Waller, 120
  first big band, 203
  Granz recordings, 32–33
  at Kansas City reunion, 203–5
  "less is more" credo, 31–32, 119
  1950s orchestra, 46–47
  sidemen on Commodore label, 128
  two-handed stride piano, 130
"Basin Street Blues," 167
"Beaujolais," 118

Bebop, 19, 85, 136
  See also Modern jazz
Bechet, Sidney, 20, 127, 150, 196
  Ellington on, 3
Beer-belly mentality, 163–64
Beiderbecke, Bix, 53, 58, 60, 108
  Cheatham's mentor, 112
  early death, 111
  on "unpredictability" of jazz, 125
Benedetti, Dean, 77
Berg, Chuck, 97
Bergman, Ingmar, 93, 95
Berigan, Bunny, 56, 108, 111
Bernardin, Father Joseph, 80
Berry, Chu, 127
Berry, Emmett, 21, 115
"Beyond category" (Ellington term), 3–4, 19, 89, 190
Big and Warm (Big Nick on India Navigation label), 134
Big bands, 25, 26–28
Bigard, Barney, 15, 23
"Billie's Bounce," 175
"Billy in the Low Ground," 183
Bing & Bob Hope (Spokane), 60
Bing and Connee Boswell (Spokane), 60
Bing & Dinah (Spokane), 59
Bing Crosby/The Crooner/The Columbia Years 1928–1934 (Columbia), 59
Bing in the Thirties (Spokane), 60
Birdland, 47, 73, 76
"Black, Brown and Beige," 6, 20, 41
"Black Beauty," 6, 41
"Black Sheep Blues," 118
Blakey, Art, 41, 80, 96, 187
  See also Art Blakey's Jazz Messengers
Blanton, Jimmy, 15
Bloom, Jane Ira, 26
"Blue Monk," 73, 90
Blue Network radio series, NBC, 123–25
Blue Note, New York, 47
"Blue Reverie," 23
"Blue Turning Grey Over You," 120–21, 122
Bluegrass music, 180–88
Blues, 158, 187, 197
  Billie Holiday and, xvii
  Charlie Parker and, 80
  Ellis on, 173
  Hodges and Parker, 19–20

ABOUT THE AUTHOR

Nat Hentoff was born in Boston, Massachusetts, in 1925. He received his B.A. with the highest honors from Northeastern University and did graduate work at Harvard University. He was a Fulbright Fellow at the Sorbonne in Paris in 1950. From 1953 through 1957 he was associate editor of *Down Beat* magazine. He was awarded a Guggenheim Fellowship in education and an American Bar Association Silver Gavel Award in 1980 for his coverage of law and criminal justice in his columns. In 1985 he was awarded an honorary Doctorate of Laws by Northeastern University.

He has published many books on jazz, biographies, education, civil liberties, and novels, including a number of books for children; and he has published for HarperCollins *Free Speech for Me—But Not for Thee: How the American Left & Right Relentlessly Censor Each Other*. In addition to his weekly *Village Voice* column, Hentoff is a columnist for the *Washington Post* and a staff writer for *The New Yorker*. He writes on music for the *Wall Street Journal*. Among the other publications in which his work has appeared are the *New York Times*, the *New Republic*, *Commonweal*, and *The Atlantic*.